The Essential Buyer's Guide

TVR
CHIMAERA
& GRIFFITH

All models 1992 to 2003

Your marque expert:
Richard Kitchen

W0017882

VELOCE PUBLISHING
THE PUBLISHER OF FINE AUTOMOTIVE BOOKS

Essential Buyer's Guides

Alfa Romeo Alfasud (Metcalfe)
Alfa Romeo Giulia GT Coupé (Booker)
Alfa Romeo Giulia Spider (Booker)
Audi TT (Davies)
Audi TT Mk2 2006 to 2014 (Durnan)
Austin-Healey Big Healeys (Trummel)
BMW Boxer Twins (Henshaw)
BMW E30 3 Series 1981 to 1994 (Hosier)
BMW GS (Henshaw)
BMW X5 (Saunders)
BMW Z3 Roadster (Fishwick)
BMW Z4: E85 Roadster and E86 Coupé including M and Alpina 2003 to 2009 (Smitheram)
BSA 350, 441 & 500 Singles (Henshaw)
BSA 500 & 650 Twins (Henshaw)
BSA Bantam (Henshaw)
Choosing, Using & Maintaining Your Electric Bicycle (Henshaw)
Citroën 2CV (Paxton)
Citroën DS & ID (Heilig)
Cobra Replicas (Ayre)
Corvette C2 Sting Ray 1963-1967 (Falconer)
Datsun 240Z 1969 to 1973 (Newlyn)
DeLorean DMC-12 1981 to 1983 (Williams)
Ducati Bevel Twins (Falloon)
Ducati Desmodue Twins (Falloon)
Ducati Desmoquattro Twins – 851, 888, 916, 996, 998, ST4 1988 to 2004 (Falloon)
Fiat 500 & 600 (Bobbitt)
Ford Capri (Paxton)
Ford Escort Mk1 & Mk2 (Williamson)
Ford Focus RS/ST 1st Generation (Williamson)
Ford Model A – All Models 1927 to 1931 (Buckley)
Ford Model T – All models 1909 to 1927 (Barker)
Ford Mustang – First Generation 1964 to 1973 (Cook)
Ford Mustang – Fifth Generation (2005-2014) (Cook)
Ford RS Cosworth Sierra & Escort (Williamson)
Harley-Davidson Big Twins (Henshaw)
Hillman Imp (Morgan)
Hinckley Triumph triples & fours 750, 900, 955, 1000, 1050, 1200 – 1991-2009 (Henshaw)
Honda CBR FireBlade (Henshaw)
Honda CBR600 Hurricane (Henshaw)
Honda SOHC Fours 1969-1984 (Henshaw)
Jaguar E-Type 3.8 & 4.2 litre (Crespin)
Jaguar E-type V12 5.3 litre (Crespin)
Jaguar Mark 1 & 2 (All models including Daimler 2.5-litre V8) 1955 to 1969 (Thorley)
Jaguar New XK 2005-2014 (Thorley)
Jaguar S-Type – 1999 to 2007 (Thorley)
Jaguar X-Type – 2001 to 2009 (Thorley)
Jaguar XJ-S (Crespin)
Jaguar XJ6, XJ8 & XJR (Thorley)
Jaguar XK 120, 140 & 150 (Thorley)
Jaguar XK8 & XKR (1996-2005) (Thorley)
Jaguar/Daimler XJ 1994-2003 (Crespin)
Jaguar/Daimler XJ40 (Crespin)
Jaguar/Daimler XJ6, XJ12 & Sovereign (Crespin)
Kawasaki Z1 & Z900 (Orritt)
Land Rover Discovery Series 1 (1989-1998) (Taylor)
Land Rover Discovery Series 2 (1998-2004) (Taylor)
Land Rover Series I, II & IIA (Thurman)
Land Rover Series III (Thurman)
Lotus Elan, S1 to Sprint and Plus 2 to Plus 2S 130/5 1962 to 1974 (Vale)
Lotus Europa, S1, S2, Twin-cam & Special 1966 to 1975 (Vale)
Lotus Seven replicas & Caterham 7: 1973-2013 (Hawkins)
Mazda MX-5 Miata (Mk1 1989-97 & Mk2 98-2001) (Crook)
Mazda RX-8 (Parish)
Mercedes-Benz 190: all 190 models (W201 series) 1982 to 1993 (Parish)
Mercedes-Benz 280-560SL & SLC (Bass)
Mercedes-Benz G-Wagen (Greene)

Mercedes-Benz Pagoda 230SL, 250SL & 280SL roadsters & coupés (Bass)
Mercedes-Benz S-Class W126 Series (Zoporowski)
Mercedes-Benz S-Class Second Generation W116 Series (Parish)
Mercedes-Benz SL R129-series 1989 to 2001 (Parish)
Mercedes-Benz SLK (Bass)
Mercedes-Benz W123 (Parish)
Mercedes-Benz W124 – All models 1984-1997 (Zoporowski)
MG Midget & A-H Sprite (Horler)
MG TD, TF & TF1500 (Jones)
MGA 1955-1962 (Crosier)
MGB & MGB GT (Williams)
MGF & MG TF (Hawkins)
Mini (Paxton)
Morris Minor & 1000 (Newell)
Moto Guzzi 2-valve big twins (Falloon)
New Mini (Collins)
Norton Commando (Henshaw)
Peugeot 205 GTI (Blackburn)
Piaggio Scooters – all modern two-stroke & four-stroke automatic models 1991 to 2016 (Willis)
Porsche 356 (Johnson)
Porsche 911 (964) (Streather)
Porsche 911 (993) (Streather)
Porsche 911 (996) (Streather)
Porsche 911 (997) – Model years 2004 to 2009 (Streather)
Porsche 911 (997) – Second generation models 2009 to 2012 (Streather)
Porsche 911 Carrera 3.2 (Streather)
Porsche 911SC (Streather)
Porsche 924 – All models 1976 to 1988 (Hodgkins)
Porsche 928 (Hemmings)
Porsche 930 Turbo & 911 (930) Turbo (Streather)
Porsche 944 (Higgins)
Porsche 981 Boxster & Cayman (Streather)
Porsche 986 Boxster (Streather)
Porsche 987 Boxster and Cayman 1st generation (2005-2009) (Streather)
Porsche 987 Boxster and Cayman 2nd generation (2009-2012) (Streather)
Range Rover – First Generation models 1970 to 1996 (Taylor)
Range Rover – Second Generation 1994-2001 (Taylor)
Range Rover – Third Generation L322 (2002-2012) (Taylor)
Rolls-Royce Silver Shadow & Bentley T-Series (Bobbitt)
Rover 2000, 2200 & 3500 (Marrocco)
Royal Enfield Bullet (Henshaw)
Subaru Impreza (Hobbs)
Sunbeam Alpine (Barker)
Triumph 350 & 500 Twins (Henshaw)
Triumph Bonneville (Henshaw)
Triumph Herald & Vitesse (Ayre)
Triumph Spitfire and GT6 (Ayre)
Triumph Stag (Mort)
Triumph Thunderbird, Trophy & Tiger (Henshaw)
Triumph TR2 & TR3 - All models (including 3A & 3B) 1953 to 1962 (Conners)
Triumph TR4/4A & TR5/250 - All models 1961 to 1968 (Child & Battyll)
Triumph TR6 (Williams)
Triumph TR7 & TR8 (Williams)
Triumph Trident & BSA Rocket III (Rooke)
TVR Chimaera and Griffith (Kitchen)
TVR S-series (Kitchen)
Velocette 350 & 500 Singles 1946 to 1970 (Henshaw)
Vespa Scooters – Classic two-stroke models 1960-2008 (Paxton)
Volkswagen Bus (Copping)
Volkswagen Transporter T4 (1990-2003) (Copping/Cservenka)
VW Golf GTI (Copping)
VW Beetle (Copping)
Volvo 700/900 Series (Beavis)
Volvo P1800/1800S, E & ES 1961 to 1973 (Murray)

www.veloce.co.uk

First published in February 2020 by Veloce Publishing Limited, Veloce House, Parkway Farm Business Park, Middle Farm Way, Poundbury, Dorchester, DT1 3AR, England. Tel 01305 260068 / Fax 01305 250479 / e-mail info@veloce.co.uk / web www.veloce.co.uk or www.velocebooks.com.
ISBN 978-1-787115-18-7 / UPC 6-36847-01518-3

Introduction
– the purpose of this book

The 1990s were unquestionably TVR's heyday. Of all the genius to emerge from the mind of then-boss Peter Wheeler, it was the Griffith and Chimaera models that went on to cement the brand well and truly in motoring's hall of fame.

Combining the curves of the existing S-Series with the V8 muscle of the outgoing 'Wedge' SE models, the Griffith was the first of the new generation to emerge from the Blackpool factory. The car would be true to the marque's DNA, featuring a GRP (fibreglass) body tub mounted to a steel tubular chassis.

Using an uprated S-Series chassis, a prototype appeared at the 1990 motor show, and by the end of the first day, people were begging Peter Wheeler to build them a Griffith of their own!

By the time Filofaxes were wearing '1992' on their covers, the subtly-revised production car appeared, now sporting discreet push-button door handles, and no fuel filler cap. There was also a new dashboard, but the biggest difference was underneath, as the S-Series-based chassis' capabilities had been deemed insufficient, should the standard 4.0 engine be upgraded. The all-new Griffith needed an all-new chassis, but at the time, TVR's only other option was that of the Wedge model – already 1970s technology.

The answer was the Tuscan challenge racer; Wheeler and his team modified this more advanced design with sensational results.

The 'Griff' garnered praise from all corners of the motoring press, and found its way onto posters adorning the bedroom walls of young petrolheads the land over

The Griffith was smooth, sleek and radical, while the Chimaera was burly and curvaceous, yet slightly more conservative in its appearance. (Courtesy S Bowden)

(including mine!). Offered with the established 3.9 (though marketed as a 4.0) Rover V8, or an in-house tuned 4.3 version (designated 400 & 430 respectively), and mated to a Rover five-speed gearbox with a limited-slip differential, it weighed in at around 1050kg (2315lb). An instant hit, the Griffith accounted for over 70 per cent of the factory's overall production in 1992 alone.

To claim the Griffith's emergence raised TVR's profile would be grossly understating things, so it came as a surprise when 'Griff' production paused in early 1993. Another master stroke was in the making, however: the new Chimaera. The cars shared both chassis and drivetrain, but the exterior designs diversified. Thanks to a fuller 'rump,' the 'Chim' boasted an even more capacious boot, which, along with slightly softer suspension, endowed it with fantastic touring abilities. Don't assume that a Griffith won't cruise the countryside, or that a Chimaera won't ignite the Stelvio Pass, though.

The Chimaera's introduction meant that in early '93, fewer Griffiths were produced. Thankfully, the Griffith did return ... and with more clout. Out were the 4.0 and 4.3 engines; instead, TVR's own in-house engineering and tuning company, TVR Power, turned the Rover V8 into a 5.0 monster, creating the Griffith 500. With 0-62mph (100km/h) achievable in little over four seconds, it probably gave rival manufacturers some sleepless nights.

With the Chimaera entering production sporting a catalytic converter, the Griffith became so-equipped on its return.

Five variants of the Rover V8 found homes in both engine bays over an 11-year production span, until the conclusion of 'RV8' production meant that the final Chimaera was produced in 2003 – the Griffith having been signed off a year earlier.

In the end, it was the Chimaera that proved the more successful of the pair, with around 6000 cars produced – over twice as many as the Griffith.

Rather than source replacement engines, TVR opted to replace both cars entirely with the new Tamora, featuring its own AJP6 engine.

With plenty of either car on the used market suiting most budgets and tastes, this guide will improve your chances of picking a great example of whichever mythically-named beast you choose, while hopefully putting some of the myths concocted about them to bed.

Thanks

This book wouldn't have been possible without the valued customers I've had at Southways Automotive. For many of the fantastic images you'll see, I owe thanks to Andy Hill at www.myfavouritephotos.com, and Jonathan Mott, who managed to assist me even when he was bitten by a snake! Thanks also to: the owners on the social media groups for their images and insight, including Jay Elle (for proving that however much you think you know about these cars, there's always something to learn); my sons Jack, Liam and Ryan for their patience when I was too busy writing to see what they'd unlocked on *Fortnite*; and finally my long-suffering wife, Natalie, for whom this book and my career in the TVR industry owe their existence.

That's a lot of V8s ... (Courtesy J Mott)

Contents

The Essential Buyer's Guide™ currency
At the time of publication a BG unit of currency "●" equals approximately
£1.00/US$1.32/Euro1.19. Please adjust to suit current exchange rates
using Sterling as the base currency.

1 Is it the right car for you?
– marriage guidance

Chimaera, or Griffith?

The market, for many, will be defined by budget (which I'll expand on in chapter 4). The sensible option is the Chimaera, which has a larger boot, is a bit more relaxed on the move, and is arguably better value for money. The Griffith is more of a poster-child; to use the term 'iconic' might be stretching it, but the only reason for choosing a Griffith over a Chimaera would be because you *want* one.

The Chimaera 400 outnumbers the Griffith 500 by nearly three to one.

Which V8 is the best V8?

If you want to wring the neck of your V8, the 4.0 or 4.3 are the happiest engines to be revved, though if you're used to fast machinery, you may find a standard 4.0 slightly lacking. The smaller displacement

For the majority who want an enjoyable weekend drive accompanied by the sound of V8 pipe music whenever the sun comes out, any version will excel.

engines are arguably the most durable of the range, though if you prefer your torque delivered violently, the 5.0 is the one for you. The 4.5 is a compromise in most respects, though there is more to consider here than performance: an engine that runs smoothly, pulls cleanly and responds crisply to your inputs can be a more rewarding drive than a one-trick pony that only goes fast.

Insurance

Many insurance companies recognise the Chimaera and Griffith as classics, and offer limited-use policies that could undercut the premium of a family saloon! Some companies require that a Category 1 or 2 immobiliser is fitted, though, so check the small print. If you're under 25 years old, you may struggle to find a company who will offer you cover, so check before looking for cars.

Will it fit in the garage?

The Chimaera is the longest, at 4015mm, while the Griffith *just* measures the widest at 1869mm, including door mirrors, which can be folded in.

Maintenance, parts availability & costs

Mechanical componentry is mostly Rover or Ford-based, but sourcing TVR-specific replacement parts is normally painless. There are a few items that might prove difficult, but no more than any other sports car of the same era.

Running costs are in-line with alternatives, but budget between ●x500-●x1000 per year for servicing/repairs with a specialist, if you cannot maintain the car yourself. Scrutinise cars that haven't been maintained at a specialist outfit, because an experienced eye is vital to good upkeep.

Controls

Both cars feature a similar swooping style dashboard and high transmission tunnel that 'cocoons' the driver.

Tall or short, slim or not-so-slim – anybody can get comfortable in one of these cars, and all models feature not only adjustable seats, but a steering wheel that adjusts for angle, and pedals for reach. Power-assisted steering was optional on most models, though none were offered with an automatic transmission.

Watching while passengers struggle to figure out how to exit your Chimaera will keep you amused for longer than it probably should.

The Griffith has marginally less storage space, though it is the only one with a proper glovebox!

Quirks

TVR used to let its cars' styling and features do all the marketing. With the Griffith, entry and exit is gained through beautifully-crafted aluminium plungers and lever, but the Chimaera's entry method varies: earlier cars featured an external plunger button, but in 1996 TVR decided door handles weren't necessary, and removed them entirely. Instead, pressing a small button located on the underside of the Citroën CX-sourced door mirrors, pops the door open. Exiting is the same for all Chimaeras, and equally brilliant: more beautifully-crafted aluminium, this time in the shape of a rotary knob, in the centre console.

You'll struggle to find the rear number plate lamps on most examples, and when

Heard a few horror stories regarding reliability? Affectionately known as 'Kermit,' this green Chimaera 400 completed possibly the longest journey ever made by a sports car, when driven 27,000 miles from the northernmost bar on the planet, to the southernmost. (Courtesy www.pub2pubadventures.com)

you require fuel, access to the filler cap is via the boot, which, of course, doesn't open with anything so casual as a handle ...

Advantages
The Chimaera offers a (slightly) roomier interior; a more capacious boot (including a wider opening making roof panel stowage easier), and a body that features what (almost) qualify as bumpers.

The Griffith doesn't really perform any single task better than the Chimaera, other than giving a slightly more visceral driving experience.

Both cars are beautiful to behold, brimming with charisma, and provide exhilarating soundtracks. They also manage to combine a supple ride with sharp handling – a balance that many manufacturers struggle to achieve, even today.

They're more reliable and durable than they're given credit for, and the majority of parts used to build them were sourced from mass-manufacturers, many of which are under-stressed.

Disadvantages
Our duo are less-suited to daily duties than they are as weekend toys. They're hand-built, they're quite demanding, and while they're a riot on the sweeping back lanes of the countryside, they can be a chore in traffic. If you're planning to use the car daily, or cover higher annual distances (5000+ miles per annum is considered high for any TVR), then be aware that these cars require upkeep that some mainstream alternatives may not.

Investment potential
We're now past the point that both models 'bottomed-out' in the market, and since 2010/11, values have been rising steadily.

With a reborn TVR due to launch an all-new incarnation of the Griffith, these cars should continue to appreciate. (Courtesy TVR Ltd)

Alternatives

Keeping to the ethos of TVR, I'd suggest that, financially, your alternatives in place of a Chimaera 400 might include BMW's Z3M or Z4 convertibles; Honda's S2000; Jaguar's XK8; the Mercedes-Benz SLK; or Porsche's Boxster. TVR's older V8S and SE Wedge models shouldn't be discounted either.

The upper echelons of either model could put you behind the wheel of a classic Mercedes-Benz SL (R107) or Morgan Plus 8; the Porsche 944 or 968 cabriolet, or, for a wildcard, one of the Cobra-replica kit cars. The Chimaera's main rival at launch was the MG RV8, which is available at this budget, as is the Marcos Mantaray (if you can find one!).

You could think closer to home and consider a later TVR, like the outrageous Tuscan, or even the car that replaced our duo: the Tamora. (Courtesy T McClean)

2 Cost considerations

– affordable, or a money pit?

Purchase
'Buy the best you can afford' is a cliché, but the Chimaera and Griffith really adhere to it. Some might say there's no such thing as a cheap TVR, only ones for which you spread the payments in repairs! This is why cars that have been maintained to schedule, and at the hands of experts, are highly desirable. Deciphering what qualifies as 'the best' isn't as straight-forward as you'd think, either, which is hopefully where this book will help. To some, the best cars might equate to those with the lowest mileage, or the most lustrous paintwork. Sadly, these models don't work like that. None of them were bad when they were brand new; it takes ignorance or neglect for them to suffer.

History is littered with previous TVR owners who "wouldn't ever buy another." Perhaps if they'd bought a good one in the first place ...

Driving it; maintaining it; repairing it
When it comes to using your TVR, thankfully, there is less risk involved. Mechanically, they're a hardy machine, and can handle aggressive driving. With a V8 up-top, fuel economy figures aren't going to give Prius drivers anything to lose sleep over, but when used for touring, 25mpg or more is realistic. If driven with more vigour, or on densely populated roads, you can naturally expect that figure to drop.

Should you find yourself unfortunate enough to possess a broken car, the costs to rectify this can vary. A hand-built car normally equates to lengthy repair times, but aside from the 'big three' (chassis, paint, interior) there's nothing too ruinous to worry about.

Some of the more significant bills you might encounter on either car, excluding the 'big three,' might include:
• Clutch renewal: ●x1000 (T-5 gearbox) or ●x2000 (Rover gearbox; an engine-out task)

Experience is key: just because the car has been routinely serviced at a garage, doesn't mean they examined all of the key areas that a TVR specialist would.

- Suspension dampers/springs: from x600 for parts, plus fitting
- Electrical gremlins: can be hard to trace on a TVR.
- Radiator: upwards of x300 for parts, or around x500 if you have to replace coolant hoses and pipes at the same time
- Exhaust manifold gaskets: x350 or more on labour, as it involves removing the whole exhaust. If it transpires that you need new exhaust components, you could spend around x2000 on a new system
- Camshaft renewal: approx x1200 for a comprehensive kit, fitted
- Tyres: you could spend up to x600 if it needs new boots

Servicing costs vary from specialist to specialist, especially as the checks they carry out can differ depending on what they feel is required, but as a rough guide:
- Minor/interim servicing: x275 to x400 yearly
- Major/full servicing: x450 to x700 every other year/three years, dependent on usage.
- Setting aside between x500 and x1000 per year for servicing and repairs is sensible if you aren't confident enough to tackle maintenance yourself.

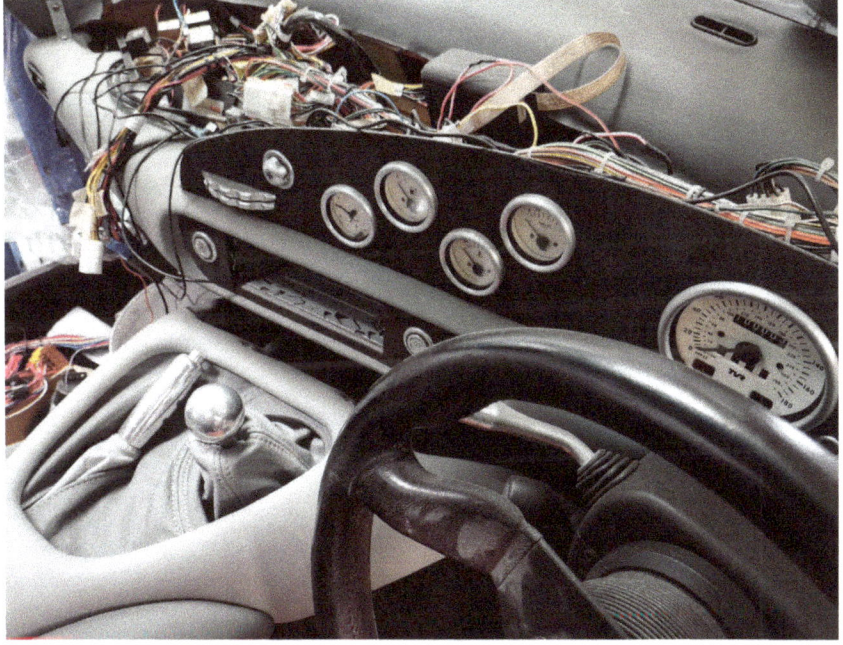

Hunt the intermittent electrical fault is not a game you want to be playing with these cars.

The Griffith and Chimaera are very agile sports cars. They're adept at cross-country cruising, but can also devour more technical sections of road on demand. They're also great touring companions, with capacious boots and an engaging driving position.

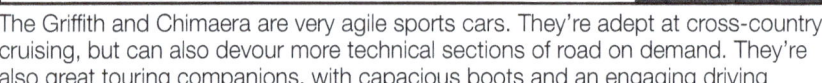

Few cars are able to dial you in to an enjoyable road like a well-sorted TVR can. (Courtesy A Hill)

One feature is a clever convertible roof design that TVR used from the Tasmin onwards. A fold-down hoop behind the driver is fixed in place by two alloy struts in front of the flexible rear screen, which lock in an 'over-centre' fashion. Positioned between this and the windscreen surround is a solid, removable targa panel, which can be either left sandwiched in tension between the rear hoop and the windscreen surround, or removed and stowed in the boot.

The targa panel can be unwieldy for some, and it's much easier to pass it into the Chimaera's wider boot opening than the Griffith's. Later Chimaeras (late '98 on) were easier still, as the bootlid was modified to open near-vertically. An absence of external hinges is a clue that a car has this feature.

Ideally, you'll have a garage to house it, as these cars can deteriorate fairly quickly when left exposed to the elements. Park up in the rain and you

TVR's desire to think 'outside the box' bestowed upon us this three-stage convertible roof design, modelled here by a Griffith 500.

might need a wetsuit to continue your journey. The cabin ventilation systems you need to restore order aren't exactly efficient, either.

There is an almost unique feeling as you drop down into their low-slung seats. The view down the bonnet is one of burly bulges juxtaposed with delicate detailing, and in traffic the car almost feels alive as the heat haze escapes from various slats and vents.

Insert the key, switch to ignition, wait for the fuel pump to prime, and turn to start. The rumble at start-up is an event in itself, though if you're not on first name terms with the neighbours, the cars still fitted with catalytic converters and standard exhausts are noticeably quieter than those with 'decats' and/ or sleeved/sports exhausts. If noise emissions are a concern, get down to a local owner's gathering; many cars are modified with 'sleeved exhausts' (more in chapter 9), so you'll be able to hear the differences.

Your chances of being allowed on a circuit or trackday are greatly reduced with a sleeved silencer, as most cars end up emitting over 105dB.

Mechanically, Chimaeras and Griffiths are robust cars. Reliability isn't a huge cause for concern, but there are a few areas where these cars suffer the odd misdemeanor. If any one aspect of the car will have you banging your head in frustration, it's likely to be the electrics, but most GRP-bodied cars are similar.

50/50 weight distribution is achieved with all

Every drive is an event, rather than just a journey.
(Courtesy P Kent)

heavy componentry within the axle-lines, providing balanced handling. Power-assisted steering was offered as an option from late '94 onwards, the presence of which aids maneuverability at low speeds, but also quickens the gearing of the rack itself. The ride is superbly damped, with taut responses and excellent body control, provided the dampers aren't tired. Of course, with all models featuring a gutsy V8 engine that doesn't need encouraging, caution is advised when applying the loud pedal, especially in the wet. Get complacent, and they can bite! ABS, traction control, airbag(s), crumple zones – all safety features these cars don't have.

You also have to bear in mind that you're in a car weighing little over 1000kg, being propelled by a large engine. Negotiating traffic and junctions requires more considered inputs than you might be used to, and the engine is only too keen to take the car away with it, whether you're ready or not. Trying to drive one around town is a bit like trying to knock a picture hook into a plaster wall using a sledgehammer.

The tardiest example will still easily crack 62mph in less than six seconds. True enough, most of today's hyper hot hatches could probably match or even better one down a drag strip, or around a circuit, but where the Chimaera and Griffith shine is in how they go fast, rather than how fast they go.

It's as good to sit in as it looks.

4 Relative values
– which model for you?

Browsing the classifieds will demonstrate that the 'Griff' generally commands higher prices than the 'Chim,' likely because fewer were produced, making it rarer today.

The earliest cars you'll find are what are known as 'pre-cat Griffs.' That is, Griffiths that were produced before the mandatory inclusion of catalytic converters in the UK in 1993.

They've a raspy V8 bark that is undiluted by decibel-sapping 'cats.' Differing visually from the later 500 model, they featured a more enclosed radiator grille, un-tinted rear indicator lights, and some exotic alloy wheels.

Ostensibly, there are no 'marks' or 'phases' to the Chimaera range. You can chronologically decipher one by appearance, but there's no crossover point between an early car, or a later one: the design simply evolved. And – for the most part – they improved in quality throughout production, with each subsequent revision appearing almost as soon as the idea was conceived. This is why you'll see some cars of the same year with differing specifications.

A limited number of Chimaera 430s were also produced. These are all early specification cars that rarely surface,

For many it will come down to what their budget will allow (I speak as someone who couldn't afford a Griffith, so once bought this Chimaera).

Offered with either a 4.0 or 4.3 engine, cars like this 1992 430 'pre-cat' model tend to be the starting point in the Griffith market.

Cars like this 1993 Chimaera 400 are where the entire Chimaera/Griffith market begins, so establish your budget early and work out what you can afford.

priced at little more than the 400s.

At the opposite end of the price scale, is the Griffith 500, which arrived shortly after. All were catalyst-equipped, though the earliest cars still feature what is known as a 'pre-serpentine' engine, which I'll cover in chapter 7. The majority will be the improved 'serpentine' engines, adding the possibility of power-assisted steering, and most cars from late 1994 onwards, be they Chimaera or Griffith, will feature the superior Borg Warner T-5 gearbox.

The 500 featured its own design of 'Estoril' alloy wheel, as well as a revised air intake/radiator grille to aid cooling. This 1994 Canadian-spec 500 is one of only two sold there. (Courtesy Z Travis)

The Chimaera 500 appeared in 1996, effectively a 'Griff' in Chimaera clothing. A rarer car, it only accounted for approximately 10 per cent of total Chimaera production.

The Chimaera spawned another option in its later life: the 450, featuring a

4.5 engine. It's generally considered a stronger, less stressed engine than that of the 500, often with little performance deficit.

The Griffith was never officially offered as a 4.5, though a handful were built in 1992 using the race-spec 450SEAC engine built by NCK Racing (later TVR Power). It's not the same engine as the Chimaera 450, and the odds of you finding a genuine one are exceptionally slim.

An approximate overview of average relative values, in ascending order of cost:

Chimaera 400 (starting point)

Is this a Griffith 430BV? Or is it a Griffith 430 with a 'BV' badge? If you believe you've unearthed a gem, speak with the TVR Car Club, or at the very least, a specialist.

Chimaera 430: 10-25 per cent increase
Chimaera 450: 30-50 per cent increase
Chimaera 500: 50-70 per cent increase
Griffith 400 (pre-cat): 40-60 per cent increase
Griffith 430 (pre-cat): 60-80 pre cent increase
Griffith 500: 90-150 per cent increase

There were a number of cars produced under various monikers signifying some kind of upgrade package or trim option. These might include:

HC 'High Compression': Effectively replacing the 430 models, this designation indicated that the engine (normally a 4.0) has been built to 500-spec (including double-valve springs, high-lift camshaft, pocketed pistons and ported heads). There are, however, reports of cars being fitted with a HC badge ... and little else. It was a cost option, so one would assume that efforts would be made to preserve the paperwork. Be suspicious if it's absent. (NB Some 500s have a '500HC' badge, while others just say '500': it's just a badge; all 500s are HC-spec.)

BV 'Big Valve': In addition to the early 4.3 engine upgrade, it was possible to specify your Blackpool rocket with the 'Big Valve' option. This consisted of hand-machining exhaust and inlet ports to engine breathing, and, perhaps unsurprisingly, bigger valves. These are rare cars, so again, check it's the genuine article.

Lastly, there are the conclusive examples. The final Chimaeras were 450s, and received faired-in headlamps; clear indicators, and seats from TVR's own Cerbera.

The final 100 Griffith 500s were designated 'SE' (Special Edition). They received the same updates, but also gained VW Corrado door mirrors; uprated

In its twilight years, the Chimaera received faired-in headlamps, just like the Griffith.

A Griffith SE is highly prized today, and priced to match. (Courtesy A Hill)

headlights; a numbered plaque containing the build number, and most distinctly of all, some unique rear lights. Most use 16in 'Estoril' wheels all round, too, as TVR's supply of 15in versions had apparently dried up.

5 Before you view

– be well informed

To avoid a wasted journey, and the disappointment of finding that the car does not match your expectations, it will help if you've planned the questions you want to ask before you make contact. Some of these points might appear basic but when you're excited about the prospect of buying your dream car, it's amazing how some of the most obvious things slip the mind ... Also check the current values in the relevant classifieds.

Where is the car?

If you wanted to find yourself a VW Golf, you'd conduct an online search within a 20 mile radius, but to find your dream TVR, you're likely going to have to travel.

The vast majority of examples will be UK-based, so even if you live in Launceston, and the car is in Lossiemouth, consider that the logistical costs involved in securing the right car are marginal compared with having to rectify the wrong car.

Dealer or private sale

The dealer has a profit to make, a warranty to cover, and, should the dealer be a TVR specialist, you can expect further premiums in return for their experience in selecting and preparing what they consider to be the best cars. Should a car appear at an independent non-TVR dealer, be alert when viewing it, because you may already know more about these cars than them.

A private sale exchanges the warranty, the cosy showroom, and the winning smile for a discount. It's fair to say that you won't receive the same legal protection as you would when buying from a dealer (though there are still legal obligations that the seller must adhere to) but the onus is on you, the buyer, to inspect it thoroughly to gauge its condition at point of sale.

It's risky business to view a car away from a private seller's home or place of work. If they want to meet somewhere neutral, or their name isn't on any of the paperwork, alarm bells should ring.

You might also find dealers selling cars on behalf of owners, known as 'sale or return': rather than the dealer buying the car for stock, an owner approaches the dealer and asks them to advertise it on their behalf. They will agree a realistic expected return with the dealer, who will then negotiate a seller's fee, and a time period over which the car will be advertised. The terms and conditions of sales like these vary from dealers who are literally just providing a forecourt and the advertising, to those almost treating it as if it were one of their own sales cars, with warranties, valeting, servicing, and more.

Reason for sale

Why is the car being sold and how long has it been with the current owner? Don't worry if the car has had a high-turnover of registered keepers: many people tend to buy cars like these as a toy. Once they've ticked their TVR box, they might go and tick a Lotus box next. Condition and paperwork to back it up are more important, though if the seller has owned (and used) the car for five years or more, that's generally a good sign.

Condition (body/chassis/interior/mechanicals)

When enquiring about a car, kick things off with the bodywork and interior. The chassis is the most critical bit, but if the seller is wary about revealing issues, they'll likely keep trying to steer the conversation back onto its stronger points, so get those out of the way. Address the paintwork (though condition is subjective, so you'll have to judge it for yourself), and ask after the interior, mechanicals (camshaft and clutch are two worth asking about), as well as when it was last serviced, and what type of service was performed (remember, time is more important than mileage, so a response of "I haven't used it" doesn't cut the mustard). Regarding the chassis, an MOT (or equivalent) guarantees nothing. You want to know how solid the outriggers and chassis rails are, how much surface rust is visible, whether any preventative maintenance has been carried out, and, if the chassis has been worked on, whether the body was, at the very least, raised to access the outriggers or not. If the chassis has been refurbished, who carried out the work, and what did they re-coat it with? In some cases, people simply re-powdercoat the chassis, resulting in a limited lifespan.

Matching data/legal ownership

Do VIN/chassis, engine numbers and licence plate match the official registration document? Is the owner's name and address recorded in the official registration documents?

For those countries that require an annual test of roadworthiness, does the car have a document showing it complies (an MOT certificate in the UK)?

If required, does the car carry a current road fund licence/licence plate tag?

Importing a TVR can be a minefield, too. Mainstream cars are fully type-approved: they conform to various emissions regulations, sport the required safety provisions, and, as such, can be used in the majority of continents without issue. TVRs, however, were produced under 'low volume type approval.' This is the reason they weren't required to be fitted with ABS or airbags, or undergo any form of crash testing. You may not be able to obtain a 'CoC' (certificate of conformity), so consult the appropriate agents first.

Does the vendor own the car outright? Money might be owed to a finance company or bank; the car could even be stolen. Several organisations can inform you whether the car has been 'written-off' by an insurance company. In the UK these organisations can supply vehicle data:
DVSA – 0300 123 9000
HPI – 0845 300 8905

The VIN plate can be located in the engine bay, on the driver's side inner wing.

AA – 0344 209 0754
DVLA – 0844 306 9203
RAC – 0800 015 6000
    Other countries have similar organisations.

Insurance/tax

Check with your existing insurer before setting out, your current policy might not cover you to drive the car if you do purchase it. In the UK, as of 2014, road fund licence cannot be transferred to the new keeper, so you'll need to tax the car too, if you want to remain on the right side of the law.

How you can pay

A cheque/check will take several days to clear and the seller may prefer to sell to a cash buyer. However, a banker's draft (a cheque issued by a bank) is a good as cash, but safer, so contact your own bank and become familiar with the formalities that are necessary to obtain one. Electronic bank

Check that the chassis' VIN corresponds with the that of the VIN plate. The chassis is the ID of the car, so make sure a previous owner hasn't switched a rusted chassis for a secondhand one, which creates registration problems. Note that on some 'pre-cat' Griffiths, the VIN plate was actually welded to a removable brace (centre picture). If you can't locate the VIN on the chassis of an early Griffith, ask questions, as the brace may have been switched with another, possibly suggesting accident damage, or even a case of mistaken identity.

transfers are normally secure, though check with your bank first for the details if you're unsure.

Buying at auction?
If the intention is to buy at auction see chapter 10 for further advice.

Professional vehicle check (mechanical examination)
There are often TVR specialists who will undertake professional examination of a vehicle on your behalf. Owners clubs will be able to put you in touch, some of whom may offer a mobile inspection service. An internet search engine is another way of finding an experienced professional.

Other organisations that will carry out a general professional check in the UK are:
AA – 0800 056 8040 / www.theaa.com/vehicle-inspection (motoring organisation with vehicle inspectors)
RAC – 0330 159 0720 / www.rac.co.uk/buying-a-car/vehicle-inspections (motoring organisation with vehicle inspectors)

Other countries have similar organisations.

Be prepared to lie on the ground to see the outriggers, and the rest of the chassis.

6 Inspection equipment

– these items will really help

This book
Reading glasses (if you need them for close work)
Magnet (a small but strong one to use on the outriggers)
Probe (a small screwdriver works well)
Overalls (or something to lay on)
Latex gloves (or similar)
Digital camera
Bright torch
A smartphone
A friend, preferably a knowledgeable enthusiast

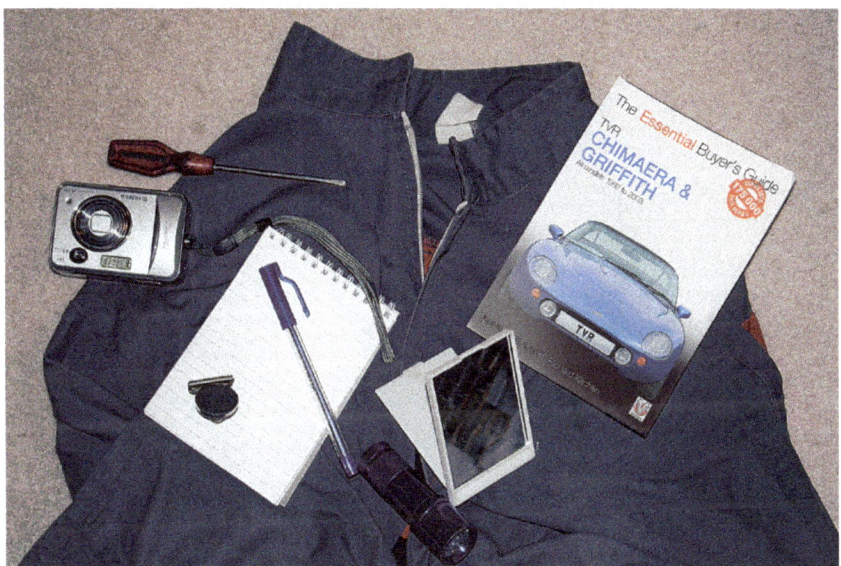

Before you rush out of the door, gather together a few items that will help as you work your way around the car. This book is designed to be your guide at every step, so take it along and use the check boxes to help you assess each area of the car you're interested in. Don't be afraid to let the seller see you using it.

Take your reading glasses if you need them to read documents and make close up inspections.

A strong (but small) magnet will assist you in checking the condition of the outriggers, particularly at the four corners. If you try to remove it and find that there's much less resistance in selected areas, it could indicate the presence of corrosion.

A small screwdriver can be used – with care – as a probe, particularly in the wheelarches on top of the outrigger tubing. With this you should be able to check an area of severe corrosion, but be careful – if it's really bad the screwdriver might go right through the tube. Wear protective gloves – underseal gets everywhere, and stains clothing.

Be prepared to get dirty. Take along a pair of overalls, if you have them, or something to lay on the floor to lie on, because if you're ill-equipped to do this, you may be tempted to forgo some crucial checks.

If you have the use of a digital camera, take it along so that later you can study some areas of the car more closely. Take a picture of any part of the car that causes you concern, and seek a friend's opinion.

A torch with fresh batteries will be useful for peering into the wheelarches and under the car (there are a lot of hard-to-see areas underneath).

You may have a smartphone that is able to provide both of the above. In addition, you'll be able to search the internet for any history of the car, including previous owners on forums. Even by simply entering the registration number into a search engine, you may learn something.

Ideally, have a friend or knowledgeable enthusiast accompany you: a second opinion is always valuable, because even if the information is right in front of you, being able to interpret needs experience. They'll likely be a 'voice of reason,' too.

This picture was taken by reaching into the wheelarch with a smartphone. See if you can spot the issue it revealed!

7 Fifteen minute evaluation
– walk away or stay?

A TVR body tub is effectively there to provide you somewhere pretty to sit, while all the important stuff goes on underneath on the chassis, so though body condition is important, it's easy to inspect as it's mostly all on the surface.

The chassis and mechanical bits aren't as easy to evaluate, so I'd suggest first looking at the exterior and interior, and checking that you're happy to continue the inspection in further detail, because either can have a significant impact on a car's value as both are costly to remedy.

The bodywork quality of either model is a progression from TVRs previous offerings. The doors should shut cleanly and with relatively even panel gaps.

TVRs feature a separate chassis and body, while most cars use a monocoque (a unitary all-in-one bodyshell).

The clever fluted leading door edge allows for quick and simple alignment.

Early Griffiths can suffer poor bootlid alignment, especially at the leading edge: worn paint is the clue here. This isn't always simple to adjust, so it's worth checking along with damage to the paint along the edge of the aperture, as the Griffith's boot opening is much tighter than the Chimaera's – the roof (aka targa panel) only just passes through.

The bonnet opening arrangement differs completely. On the Chimaera, it's a simple rearwards opening, lifting from the base of the windscreen. It simply hinges on two 8mm studs located in the underside of the bonnet nose, which are attached to a rose joint on either side of the aperture on the body. These studs take the entire weight of the bonnet, and when opened on a windy day have to deal with the bonnet doing its best impression of a sail. It's very common to find the studs have detached, causing a wobbly bonnet. A lasting repair isn't a quick fix. The Griffith features a more complex arrangement whereby it pops open at the rear as per the sister car, before raising slightly, and then rolling rearwards. This allows the tapered nose of the bonnet – normally sunk below the bodywork – to slide on a pair of nylon bearings until it's clear of the nose, at which point the front then lifts. Think of it as a classic BMW 'sharknose' layout, only reversed. Check for scratches and chips at the point where the nylon bearings (just) clear the opening.

Remember, you're looking for things that are potentially costly to rectify, because if you buy the car, it's you who's going to bankroll it. Star crazes in the GRP, or subtle gel coat fractures, scratches, faded paint, flaking lacquer, excessive stonechips, poor accident repairs, etc, are all potential financial headaches. TVR's factory paint shop was operated by a talented workforce, so a poor paint finish is likely an indication that the car has been repainted since. The windscreens are difficult to remove without damaging, too, meaning they often get left in place during repairs, so gently pee mk under the edge of the rubber trim if you suspect paintwork repair is present; some of the cut-price outfits won't make an effort to hide the masking lines, and GRP cars are prone to microblistering if not painted in the correct conditions, which is not only a condition that will worsen over time, but one that might require the costly stripping back of all paintwork to start from scratch.

Don't forget to consider the colour scheme of the car itself, either, because TVR offered a multitude of hues as an option, and would likely agree to any shade you desired, should you line their palms with enough silver. Great! But how easy would it be to match that pearlescent yellow should the car require future repair work? You don't want a simple blow-over of the nose to look mismatched, or worse, turn into a full respray. TVRs are curvy cars, so walk around the car, looking for poor colour matches. Try it again at different angles, and in different lights.

Another hint that the car might have been involved in a body repair, is around the clear lenses that cover the headlights (Griffith and last Chimaeras), and rear lamps (Chimaera only). These left the factory with a neat bead of sealant and black edging, but untidy repairs usually result in lenses that fog up, and covers that don't fit properly.

Lastly, check the roof for wear and damage to the roof panel itself, which is vulnerable when stowed in a tightly-packed boot, while the rear screen stitching at the edges can fail and the screen itself can split, particularly near the alloy struts.

There's a technique to collapsing the roof without trapping the screen, so if the seller lovingly places a rolled up beach towel inside the rear window as they fold it down, that's not a sign of madness.

Like the paintwork, TVR would pretty much build any interior you paid them

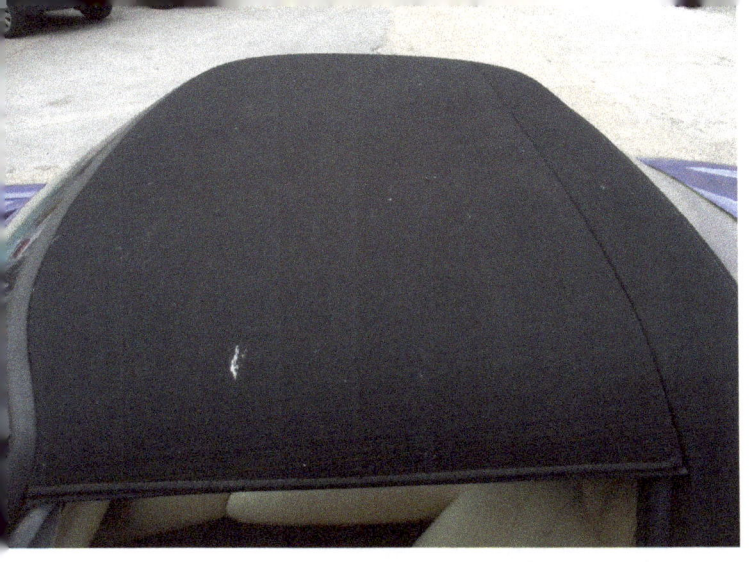

The roof fabric itself is durable, though it sometimes deteriorates along the trailing edge of the side windows, just above the door.

to. Plenty of customers had taste (they were buying a TVR, after all!). However, some were a little more 'individual' than others, so occasionally you'll find some bold colour combinations. If you fall in love with it, great, nothing to concern yourself with. However, if you've a selection of cars you're looking at, ask yourself how tricky it might be to sell the car later on, or whether, for example, purple leather with orange striping would affect your own enjoyment of the car.

Once you've finished channelling your inner Kelly Hoppen, look around for faded or damaged carpet, often caused by UV rays or water ingress in the footwells (try tipping the seats forwards to reveal the intended colour of the carpet). Most 'Griffs' and 'Chims' came with what was known as a 'half-hide' interior, where the face of the seats and possibly one or two areas of trim were leather, but the dashboard, centre console seat backs and door card surrounds were a matching (or contrasting) vinyl. In such cars, the vinyl can actually wear better than leather, as the latter requires more care to maintain condition, but check the colours still match. A lower number of cars were specified with full-leather interiors, which was

a cost option. Inspect the upholstery for crazing, cracking or hardening, as well as traces of glue.

The majority of these cars featured a metal dash panel with a veneer fascia, within which dials, gauges and most of the switchgear were housed, but this can fracture over time.

Re-veneering is a skilled trade, and doesn't come cheap. For that reason, many cars will have an alternative fitted, such as brushed aluminium (some of which were available aftermarket), carbon fibre or, if you're unlucky, faux carbon fibre. You may also find cars with the original metal panel simply covered in a vinyl wrap, or the bare metal panel itself highly polished.

The later examples of either model tended to come with a textured alloy dash from the factory, in keeping with the more contemporary styling direction TVR's newer models were taking. In either car, there were some alterations on the switchgear fitted, mainly splitting the two models into 'early' and 'later' versions. All share the same steering wheel

Lucretius once wrote "One man's meat is another man's poison." Could he have been referring to TVR interiors?

It's quite common for the veneer to be cracked or flaking, so check it all closely, particularly around the heater and lighting controls on the Chimaera, and the air vents and radio on the Griffith.

With any metal dash, such as in this 2001 Chimaera 450, check the sun's reflection doesn't dazzle you when driving with the roof off!

options, with the ignition key and column stalks from a Vauxhall Cavalier. These can differ visually, as many cars will feature aluminium levers, which are still the same component, just modified. In some cases, cars left the factory with them (such as the Griffith SE), but in many cases these will be one of the few alternatives produced aftermarket, often sold in a package with gear knobs, handbrake lever handles, vent surrounds and ash tray facings.

Pay close attention to the inner edges of the dashboard, as, if the veneer panel has been removed, it's very easy to graze the taut edges of the material, and the dashboard is a time-consuming piece to remove, retrim and refit.

Now inspect the beauty beyond skin depth. This is probably the trickiest area to assess, but also potentially the least important (of the main areas I've mentioned). The reason is that the Rover V8 may not be a technological tour de force, but it is a proven unit. Unless somebody has been very busy, all cars will be fitted with one, so the majority of mechanical areas to assess are virtually the same throughout. As mentioned previously, there are the earlier pre-serpentine engines, and the later serpentine engines.

The term serpentine, or 'serp' as it's often referred to, relates to the engine's drivebelt layout: the 'pre-serp' cars use a conventional V-belt as you'd find on nearly all cars dating back to prewar.

It drives the alternator and water pump from the crankshaft pulley, and is tensioned manually. These engines were fitted from launch, up until late 1994. As with all TVRs, it's a fluid changeover date: ten serp-engined cars might have been produced before another pre-serp car left the line, so don't be too concerned if you find a younger car with the older engine, while you might find some cars have been converted.

Serp engines use a flat 'multi-rib' belt, as per modern cars,

The pre-serp drivebelt setup, which was phased out in 1994.

The serpentine drivebelt setup was introduced during 1994, and was standard fitment from 1995 onwards. Note the difference in the belt width/shape, and relocation of the coolant swirl pot, behind which the power-steering pump will be fitted (if applicable).

which is able to run on both the grooved side, and the smooth side, snaking its way around the various pulleys (hence 'serpentine'), allowing it to drive more ancillaries with a single belt.

This belt is tensioned using a spring-loaded arm with an idler pulley wheel, and it's this more compact layout that allows the addition of a high-pressure power steering pump (as the pump the pre-serp uses for other models – such as TVR's Wedge – sits where the exhaust is routed on a Chim/Griff). It's important to note, however, that all serp engines feature the drive pulley for a PAS pump (located behind the coolant swirl point); on unequipped cars, it's simply an idler pulley. If power steering is fitted on a car you're viewing, check for leaks around the rack itself. These racks can be an expensive repair if they fail.

Serp engines aren't just about the drivebelt, however. The later engine has an uprated oil pump setup where it is directly driven by the crankshaft rather than by the camshaft via the distributor, and regarded as being tougher. That's not to say the pre-serp is a weak engine; it's just the serpentine engine is an evolution of it, and is generally considered more preferable for the more up-to-date design.

You're unlikely to uncover any serious issues with the engine in most versions, though the 5.0 is considered the most delicate, perhaps understandably, as it's the most highly tuned. It can be susceptible to piston slap, normally identifiable as a quiet, lightweight 'chattering' noise on the static overrun. The 4.5 is effectively the same block as the P38 Range Rover (which was marketed as a 4.6), and was developed post-BMW's takeover of MG Rover. It's normally considered the strongest engine, due to larger crankshaft journals, and bearing caps that are cross-bolted, though issues with porous block castings on the P38 have been documented over

The easiest way to visually determine whether a car has the optional PAS (in case the description fails to mention it), is the presence of the fluid reservoir on the right-hand engine bank, just behind the ignition coil.

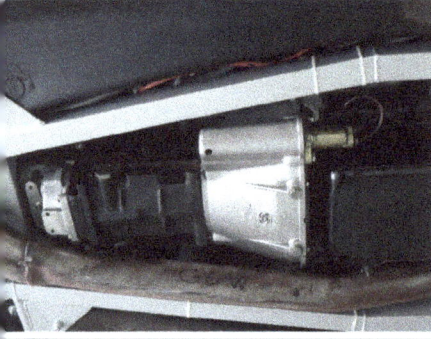

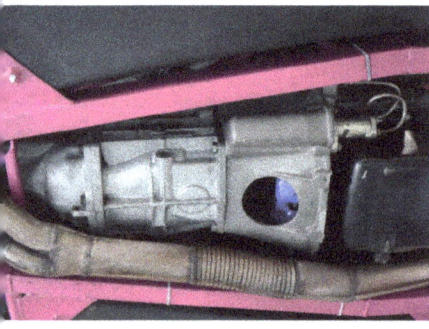

the years, so this is also a potential issue on the 4.5 Chimaera. It's worth pointing out, however, that the reported issues with the Range Rover are stemming from cars in daily use, presumably covering 10,000-12,000 miles per year. Your average TVR manages far less than that. Companies such as V8 Developments are well-versed in remedying this issue.

Though the RV8 can suffer big mechanical problems (as can any engine), the common issues to look for are leaking exhaust manifolds and gaskets, oil leaks and worn camshafts, but it'll be quite difficult to decipher the latter of those on the road, unless it's very worn.

On cars fitted with the LT77 gearbox, clutch replacement is an engine-out job, and costly as a result. It's much easier on a T5 car, but still worth checking that the biting point isn't at the very top of the pedal travel. Clutch kits on the bigger-engined variants are uprated from the stock RV8 items, and quite costly to purchase in comparison to the 400.

Two types of limited-slip differential were used throughout production. Earlier versions used a GKN device, which was fitted regardless of engine size until it was phased out by a BTR unit around 1996. There's no 'right' or 'wrong' choice here; both have their pros and cons. The GKN uses a Torsen (torque-sensing) limited-slip setup, providing the flexibility of an 'open' differential at low speeds, but with superior control and distribution when you need it. The BTR is still a mechanical LSD, but it's of the more conventional 'cone' friction type, and can be slightly slower to react to your

Earlier cars have Rover LT77 gearboxes (silver chassis), which have reverse in the top-left of the gate; most cars will be T5-equipped, with reverse in the bottom-right. The T5 gearbox (purple chassis) is preferable as it's stronger and lighter, and generally has a more precise shift action. It's also less labour-intensive to renew the clutch.

inputs. On the flipside, the BTR is considered stronger, while replacement parts are easier to source than on the GKN unit. Both are susceptible to oil leaks, and – on the last cars fitted with the GKN (95-96) – have a rear cover plate with a filler plug that is very difficult to access. As a result, there's a strong chance an oil change or two has been skipped over the years, so check the maintenance records to see who it has been entrusted to.

Chassis, chassis, CHASSIS! This is the battlecry you'll likely hear from most owners. It's not that the chassis is a difficult component to repair or overhaul, but is a time-consuming and therefore costly exercise, and, as a result, is not one most owners are looking to get involved in.

Another issue is that should a car require chassis work, there will undoubtedly

In 1996, the GKN Tor-Sen differential was phased out for the BTR 'cone' type: the former is identifiable by a backplate with a smooth case, and substantial heatsink finning. The BTR has ribbing on the case, but a smooth backplate.

be a host of other components that are worn out and require renewal at the same time, such as suspension bushes and dampers, brakes, clutch, coolant hoses/pipes, and potential wiring headaches, which can push the cost higher and higher.

The last consideration is that just because the chassis is advertised as having received attention, that doesn't mean it's been carried out satisfactorily. Plenty of owners try to cut costs, and in doing so, cut corners. I've seen some truly shocking 'repairs' throughout my career, including a car with rusty tubes cloaked in fibreglass matting (complete with sealant shaped to replicate welds), and one car with sections of a child's climbing frame glued to the remains of rusted outriggers.

The outriggers are the area most people concern themselves with, but this isn't the full picture. Yes, the outriggers are the most susceptible to corrosion, and they do tend to rot first. However, there are areas of the main chassis that also rot, and these are much trickier to correct, so a car listed as having 'new outriggers' fitted, needn't necessarily be a better candidate than a car without; in some instances, I'd be more attentive in looking for problems. It's all down to condition, and I'll explain how to closely inspect the chassis in Chapter 9.

Remember, only buy a car from an individual who can prove that they are the person named in the car's registration document (V5C in the UK) and, preferably, at the address shown in the document. Also check that the VIN or chassis number and engine numbers of the car match the numbers in the registration document.

Don't get bogged down thinking the only vulnerable parts of the chassis are those closest to the ground. This tube lurks below the exhaust manifolds, and is often the worse for wear.

www.velocebooks.com / www.veloce.co.uk
Details of all current books • New book news • Special offers

8 Key points
– where to look for problems

You know how much the car is advertised for, and you can guesstimate approximate running costs such as insurance, maintenance and fuel, but what about the unknowns? How could a car advertised for ●x15,000 end up costing you more than a ●x25,000 car?

The trend you need to follow here, is future proofing: putting on your most pessimistic hat, and thinking about what costs you're likely to encounter with the car in question, because the speed at which your dream could turn into your worst nightmare can almost be as rapid as the cars themselves.

Chassis
The chassis is undoubtedly the most costly thing to correct, if needed. All chassis were fabricated and powdercoated at the Bristol Avenue factory, and came in three different factory colours, which were:
Silver: 1992-approx 1996
White: 1997-approx 2000
Light grey: 2000-end of production

Cars fitted with the earlier silver chassis seem to fare better in the fight against rust, and in my experience I've found the cars with white chassis to normally be the more likely to suffer with corrosion in the main chassis. There's no 'hard and fast' rule, however, so assume nothing.

Quick outrigger replacements tend to start at around ●x1800, but if you want to have the chassis restored properly, you could easily spend more than ●x7000 at a specialists, especially if you have additional (and likely required) mechanical work carried out at the same time.

Bodywork
GRP is more labour intensive than regular steel bodywork, and it takes a

Chassis issues can often be hidden: this outrigger looked solid during a prior inspection at an independent establishment, but with the body removed it was a different story.

Believe it or not, this is the same chassis as above. It can cost nearly the total value of the car to achieve, however.

Specialist bodyshops charge specialist prices, so check the bodywork for damage, cracking, and crazing.

specialist bodyshop to get good results. A high-quality full-body respray can often cost ●x4000 or more on a car such as this, should the current paintwork be exceptionally bad, or you find microblisters. Remember, if the bodywork has some questionable areas of finish, more may develop as time passes.

Interior

A full re-trim at a professional trimmer can be ●x3000 or more, so make sure the interior is either in good order, or the car is priced to reflect it. The quality of materials varied over production, and some age better than others.

9 Serious evaluation
– 60 minutes for years of enjoyment

You're not looking to buy one of these cars for practical purposes; It's purely a matter of your heart guiding your head! Restore some rationale by scoring the car in each of the following areas, with a score of '1' equating to an area needing repair; '2' being an area that is serviceable, but will need attention in the near future; '3' being an area that presents no immediate issues, and '4' being pristine; needing no attention at all, other than upkeep.

Body (general issues)

Check everywhere for star cracks; microblisters; colour mismatches and poor repairs. Scratches and cracks can appear anywhere, particularly the nose which, being so low, is susceptible to stone chipping. Check for signs of scrapes or scuffs along the base of the doors, as their low height can lead to contact with kerbs, as well as along the trailing edge, in case there has been contact with garage walls. Check the entire surface and edges of the bonnet for crazing or cracking. Chimaeras are particularly sensitive to lacquer peel, especially around the front indicator recesses, but check everywhere for signs of flaking.

Bonnet

The Chimaera's biggest issue is those hinges at the front. Open the bonnet and check for lateral movement; If detected, inspect the hinges closely. Should the threaded studs be loose, the mounting has failed, and that's not a simple fix. While there, inspect the condition of the protective heat-reflective matting on the underside, which often peels away. On the Griffith, check for damage to the paint around the front edge of the opening, as the nylon rollers pass closely when opening or shutting, while the trailing edge of the bonnet can also suffer, as on some cars it's been known for the bonnet to foul the wiper arms. Finally, check the bonnet stay mechanism and its mounting, as the original is known to fail.

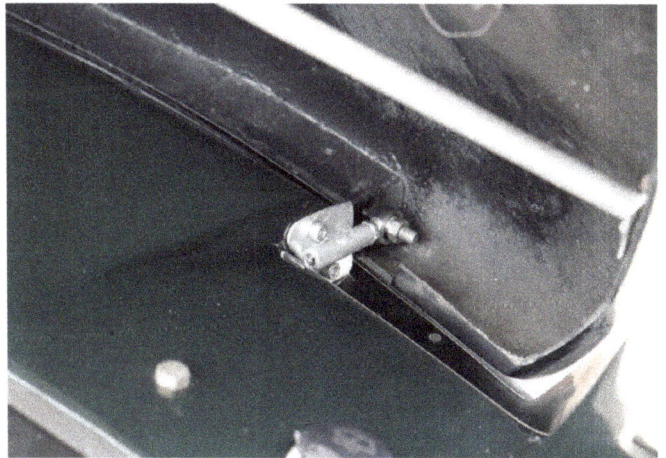

A lot of strain is heaped upon the small studs mounted in these rosejoints, so check they're still solidly anchored to the Chimaera's heavy bonnet.

Engine bay

The heat-reflective matting panels, which should cover the lower bulkhead (above the gearbox bellhousing), as well as the inner wings, can suffer heat damage from the exhaust manifolds, and fail to protect the body adequately.

Though a seemingly trivial area to inspect, locate the round black cover beside the brake fluid reservoir on the inner wing, under which the clutch master cylinder is located. The tidiness with which the sealant has been applied to this cover is a good indication as to the level of care the car has received.

Roof

Focus on the edges of the targa panel, which can become damaged and frayed with the continual removal and refitting it endures, along with the

The exhausts sit in close proximity to the fibreglass body, so the protective heat-lining needs to be intact to perform its job. Look for scorched carpets in the footwell if you suspect a failure.

The targa roof panel should fit neatly and securely. Check for wear to the covering, particularly along the edges where the fabric is tauter. The underside is a lacquered carbon fibre finish – beware of ugly 'home-made' versions!

fabric near the hinge of the rear fold-up section, as this often becomes detached from the frame. A car laid up outside for long periods of time could exhibit stains from moss and mildew.

Check the rubber seals for signs of damage, and the rear screen for perforation, cracking, or a cloudy appearance caused by UV damage and/or unsuitable cleaning products. Check the finish with which the rear screen is sewn in; TVRs should have neat, straight stitching.

Door mirrors   4 3 2 1

The majority of 'Chims' and 'Griffs' are fitted with Citroën CX units. These cannot be installed to the door as Citroën designed, so have to be installed after assembly, which sometimes results in ill-fitting mirrors (made obvious by the mirrors sitting at different angles left to right). These cars often live in single garages, and have their mirrors continually folded in and out far more than would have been expected of the average French saloon of the 1980's. As a result, the metal bracket connecting the mirror body to the door can fracture, and replacement is a fairly involved job. Not a reason to walk away from a car, but check the mirrors aren't 'floppy,' and that they 'lock' into their positions while folding. Check also that the paint isn't damaged on the surface of the door, where the mirror has been folded in. The very last cars have VW Corrado mirrors fitted, as per the Cerbera and subsequent 'T-cars.'

Lighting   4 3 2 1

On all cars, check the security and finish of the perspex lenses that cover any applicable exterior lamps. On the Chimaera in particular, check the headlamps themselves to ensure the internals are bright and reflective and do not display a brown tint behind the glass, as these units are not sealed and can corrode as a result. Any afflicted units need stripping down and replacing, which is a costly exercise.

Electric windows   4 3 2 1

These can be slow in operation due to tired motors, poor alignment, wiring issues, or all three combined. With the roof up, check that the glass slides up and down freely, and that the pane itself is free of scratches. Depending on how tight a fit the window is, the rubber seals fitted to the roof that run up the trailing edge of the window can become damaged over time, as can the top of the rubber door seal, just below.

Windscreen   4 3 2 1

Inspect the windscreen for chips, damage and delamination around the edges. Replacements aren't always easy to source, and many owners experience issues having them fitted. Check the surrounding interior trim for any damage that has occurred, which may indicate the screen has been replaced, especially the lower rubber seal, which may have been torn out and simply glued back in above the perforated scuttle trim panel, which itself needs checking for signs of damage or distortion as it is fiddly to remove, and often prevents access to components such as the throttle cable; Check a previous repairer hasn't lost patience with it.

Seats & upholstery   4 3 2 1

The most obvious concern is the condition of the leather and vinyl-trimmed covers.

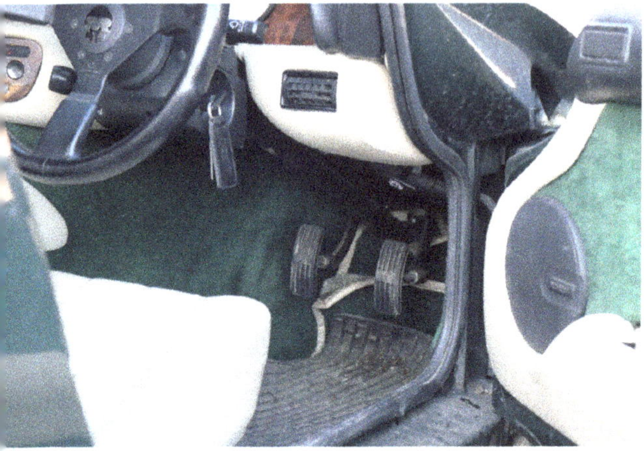

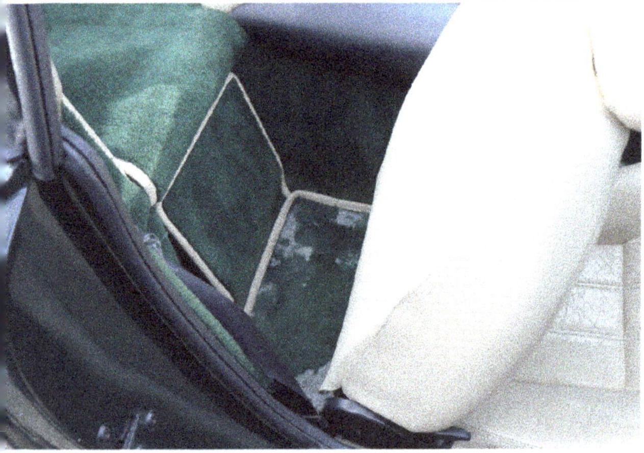

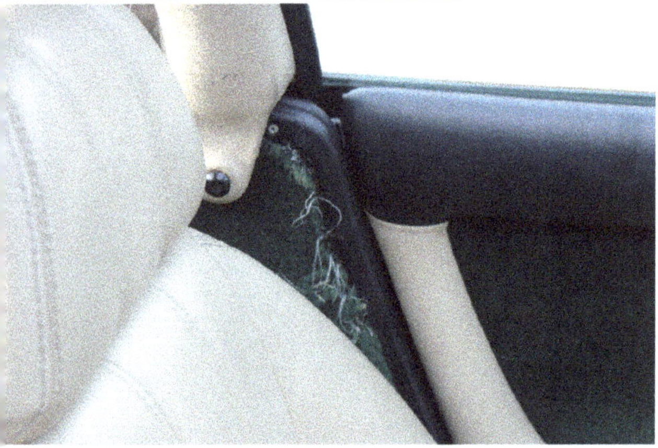

Replacements alone can cost x500 or more, and there is always the risk the colours won't match the remaining trim. If you suspect either seat is sagging, it's possible the wires in the base have corroded and broken. Either seat should slide freely back and forth on its runners, and should lock securely.

Carpets

Many cars will feature a two-tone interior, with contrasting hues between selected pieces of trim. Check everywhere, especially the rear 'parcel shelf'; along the sides of the transmission tunnel, and down the back of the seats. While down the back of the seat, check for areas that receive little in the way of UV rays, compared with areas that are constantly basking in sunlight, as well as evidence of rainwater

Inspect the interior throughout: areas of the carpet normally in the shade will give a key as to how badly it has faded; check the piped edging for frayed stitching, and all over for excess glue, mould and damp stains caused by leaks.

leaks, or mould. The quality of materials in these interiors varied over the years, and some are more sensitive to colour fading than others.

Beware poor quality retrims. Look for loose carpet, especially in the footwells and under the dash. In the driver's footwell in particular, as loose carpet behind the pedals might suggest a brake or clutch fluid leak.

Electrics

A GRP body doesn't possess a natural earth, so many circuits have twice as much wiring as you would normally find, which increases the likelihood of problems. It also means that any DIY-approaches to repairs or accessories should be inspected more closely than with a metal-bodied car. Some of the connectors in the engine bay have a hard life, such as the ones on the cooling fan switch, lambda sensors and fuel pump. If battery charge or jump start connectors are visible, ask some questions; These are simple cars, electronically, so if a battery needs topping up in the short-term, there is likely a power drain.

Alarm/immobiliser

The majority of cars up to the mid-nineties were fitted with a Foxguard system, many of which have since been replaced. Later, TVR switched to Meta systems, which as a component is a reliable cat. 1 system. However, TVR inexplicably wired the interrupter circuits in the wrong way around, meaning the starter circuit can fail once the starter motor starts to wear and draw more current. This issue is exacerbated when the engine is hot (research TVR 'hot start problem'). Many cars will feature a 'hot start kit', but this is effectively just a bypass circuit with additional relay. Newer Meta replacements have been configured to rectify the incorrect wiring circuit.

Check all fobs are present, that the system arms/disarms correctly, and that the doors locks actuate with the central locking.

Speedometer/ gauges

A few iterations of instrument were used, but the vast majority of cars will have Caerbont gauges, identifiable as having a silver aluminium bezel, with a white face/ black markings, or black face/white markings. For the most part, the gauges are reliable, but the odometer can suffer

Later updated Meta security systems like this combined key and fob indicate that the existing system has already been replaced. 9/10 owners opt to replace older faulty systems with this newer version. A separate black fob is more likely in an early variant.

from sticking drums, despite the speedometer continuing to function. This normally occurs when the last three digits are '999', but is also known to trigger at '099'. Look around the edge of the silver ring bezel for signs of distortion, as this needs removing in order to access the internals. Check the mileage history through the old MoTs (or equivalent) for signs that a car has covered very few miles between tests (if any!). If any of the recorded entries end with a '99' or '999', there is a chance the odometer ceased to function at some point, and the indicated mileage may not be true. The latest cars featured a digital odometer, which doesn't suffer this issue.

NB It's worth pointing out this isn't an assertion that the seller is acting unscrupulously; they may well not be aware themselves. Small discrepancies don't necessarily mean the car is no longer worth pursuing, as condition is more important than mileage covered.

MOT Date	Odometer	+/- Diff	
04 May 2006	74,100		▶
17 Jul 2007	77,999	+3,899	▶
11 Jul 2008	78,502	+503	▶
06 Aug 2009	79,000	+498	▶
04 May 2010	79,800	+800	▶
06 May 2011	81,094	+1,294	▶
14 Apr 2012	81,600	+506	▶
09 Mar 2013	83,700	+2,100	▶
08 May 2014	83,999	+299	▶
20 Jul 2015	83,999	+0	▶
11 Apr 2019	84,000	+1	▶

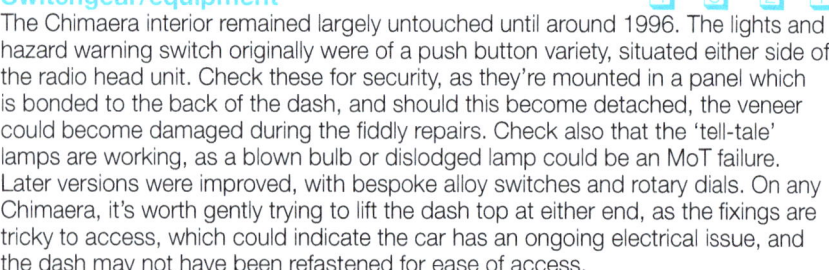

Mileage Data

Searching through the vehicle's MOT history is worthwhile, as the odometers are prone to sticking, meaning the mileage displayed may not reflect the mileage covered. There are many apps available on smartphones that can do this, often for little or no charge.

Switchgear/equipment

4 3 2 1

The Chimaera interior remained largely untouched until around 1996. The lights and hazard warning switch originally were of a push button variety, situated either side of the radio head unit. Check these for security, as they're mounted in a panel which is bonded to the back of the dash, and should this become detached, the veneer could become damaged during the fiddly repairs. Check also that the 'tell-tale' lamps are working, as a blown bulb or dislodged lamp could be an MoT failure. Later versions were improved, with bespoke alloy switches and rotary dials. On any Chimaera, it's worth gently trying to lift the dash top at either end, as the fixings are tricky to access, which could indicate the car has an ongoing electrical issue, and the dash may not have been refastened for ease of access.

Most Griffiths use complex electro-solenoids to operate heating and ventilation. The pre-cat models use a rotary switch for fan speed, but a pair of what appear to be electric window switches, mounted horizontally, to operate the heater valve and direction flaps. It's not a particularly user-friendly system, but all of this is academic as the blower motor is located down behind the nearside headlamp, and struggles to produce enough air to reach the cabin anyway. Check this, along with the cross-pipe under the bonnet that runs from left to right footwell vents, as if it isn't sealed, you'll be on the receiving end of some unpleasant fumes from the engine bay.

Later Griffiths were much improved, with four alloy rotary dials, while the 500SE model borrowed the Chimaera's simple (but more effective) switchgear.

Alloy wheels

Chimaeras mainly feature 'Imola' five-spoke wheels, while the 'Estoril' (as fitted to Griffith 500s) was fitted to the Chimaera 500, and was optional on the later 400 & 450 models. Inspect the edges of the rims for kerb damage, and, in the case of the Imola rims, check the inner edges of the spokes for signs of yellow primer, as the paint was sometimes applied thinly here. 'Estorils' use flush-fitting centre caps to cover the wheel nuts, secured with a single security bolt, which, if over-tightened, can crack the plastic cover. Check that the removal key is present in the tool bag, too.

The pre-cat Griffith was offered with more exotic rims, though they're harder to preserve. A chiseled five-spoke, originally known as the 'Camille,' by Gotti, later produced by AMIL, or OZ Racing lattice-style cross-spokes, with a split rim. Both wheels use a polished or diamond-cut lip, which deteriorates over time. If you find

(Clockwise from top left): 'Camile' five-spoke as fitted to pre-cat Griffiths; OZ Racing cross-spoke split rims fitted to pre-cat Griffiths; 'Estoril' design as fitted to all '500' models (was also a cost option on the entire Chimaera range); 'Imola' five-spoke as fitted to the majority of Chimaeras.

Ithe wheels have been fully coated or painted, it may be because they're too corroded and pitted underneath to recover, so bear that in mind if you want the original 'pre-cat' look (and who wouldn't; they're stunning!).

If you happen to drive a car with larger aftermarket wheels fitted, be aware that low profile tyres can make them more 'unsettled' to drive on poorly surfaced roads.

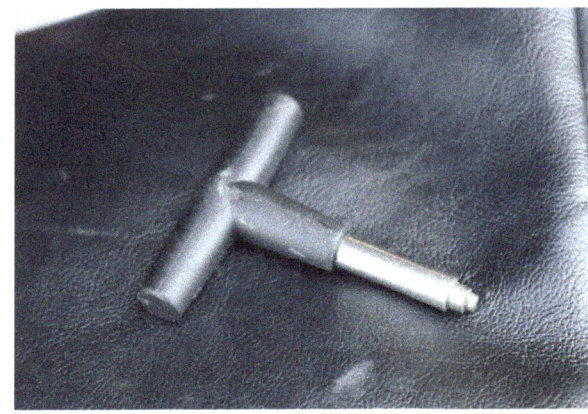

In the boot, there should be a 'space saver' spare wheel, though these are often removed to boost luggage space. Make sure it's been put back. Cars also came with a black vinyl bag for the targa roof panel, another smaller one to house items such as the jack, wheel brace, locking wheel nut key (if fitted) and security bolt key for the centre caps on cars fitted with such (early OZ lattice-style and 'Estoril' versions of the 500 models).

Tyres

The dimensions themselves vary depending on specification, but more likely to be an issue is the date of manufacture. Normally, tyre wear is the most common

From 2000, the vast majority of tyres have a date-of-manufacture stamp. Worth checking, because these cars often cover low annual mileages, so the tyres might need replacing, even if there is plenty of tread left!

cause for replacement, but on an occasionally used car, the main issue is the rubber becoming hard due to age. Look for a date stamp comprised of four digits (XX=week; YY=year): anything over 6 years old should be scrutinised for cracking or signs of perishing, though cars that have been regularly garaged, out of the sun's UV rays will fair better.

Suspension bushes

Cars produced after 1997 were fitted with nylon thrust washers to prevent the bush failing laterally, and while TVR also retrofitted them to some earlier cars during maintenance, many cars won't have them today due to them breaking and falling out, or being misplaced during repairs. If they're missing, check the clearance between the various chassis eyelets and corresponding suspension arms. There should be an even gap each side; If not, the bush has started to 'walk.' This is more likely to be the cause of a failed bush than of excess play, as the standard bushes are very stiff, and there isn't much rubber to perish.

Consider also that the cost to refresh all the suspension bushes is not always the whole story; the fixing bolts sometimes rust into the bush sleeves, so removal involves cutting the arms away. In the event that you do successfully remove all the suspension arms, you might find them heavily rusted, so what started as a suspension bush change is now some rusty suspension wishbones that need replacing. That's the line of thinking you need to take with most things fixed to the chassis, because this is typical of how costs on older cars escalate. If the car has polyurethane bushes fitted, inspect them for condition and type: the best ones also use thrust washers, but some of the cheaper options use a 'cotton-reel' design, and these don't tend to last.

Note the non-existent gap on the left of this wishbone mounting, and the excessive gap on the right: the gaps should be even, but cars running without thrust washers each side is prone to this issue, which is really the only way these bushes fail.

Dampers/ride height

4 3 2 1

Checking the bushes at the top and bottom of the dampers, too. Some pre-cat Griffiths were fitted with Koni dampers (which rode beautifully). These have a red body, while the majority of cars were kitted out with Bilsteins (early – green body/ later – yellow). It's likely they'll have been replaced by now, normally with items that are adjustable for ride height, damping, or both. If the car is fitted with adjustable dampers, but doesn't handle terribly well or rides poorly, it may need adjustment. In order to do that, check that the spring seats aren't rusted, and that the damping adjusters move freely. If the car is sitting unusually low, pay close attention to the exhaust system and engine sump for signs of damage.

Steering

4 3 2 1

Starting down at the rack, check the inner tie rods for any play as they enter the rack, as any play could be the rack itself. Check also for play at the pinion shaft; the upper and lower universal joints on the lower part of the steering column, and the bulkhead bearing, which is accessible in the driver's wheelarch. On the test drive, it

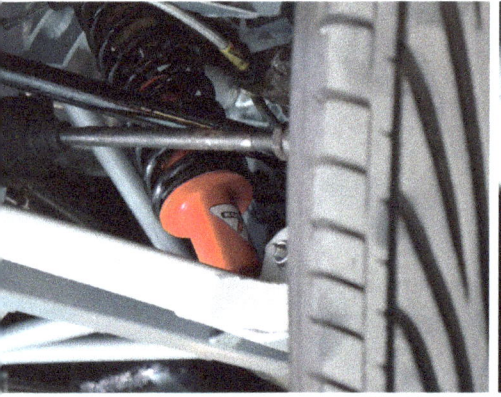

Not all dampers will look this good! OE options including the red Konis were only fitted to very early examples of either model, while the majority received Bilstein, identifiable by a yellow or green (as seen here) body. The alternative is an adjustable unit, which many cars will have been fitted with, though check these are still serviceable and that the various adjusters aren't seized or faulty if the dampers look old.

If the alloy casing of the power steering rack's pinion valve is covered in oil or grease, it could indicate a leaky seal. In this image, note the wiring connector for the right-hand lambda sensor dangling perilously close to the steering joint!

should track straight and true, with a reasonable amount of self-centre action, and little to no play when stationary.

Power steering reservoir & leaks (if fitted)

Dip a white piece of paper in the fluid – it should stain red. If the fluid in the reservoir is black, it suggests that the hoses are perishing internally, and contaminating the fluid, which in turn can damage components in the system. At minimum, it needs new hoses, pipes and a flush.

A damp pinion body indicates deeper problems, as the visible seal is one of two present, and only designed to prevent dirt reaching the inner one.

Check the pump doesn't groan excessively while hard lock is applied. A degree of whine is normal, but excessive groaning; creaking or rumbling is not.

Brake/clutch fluid leaks and servo

While on the trail of pedal-related componentry, have a look in the footwoll at the pedals where they attach to the various linkages and components. Any signs of fluid leakage from either master cylinder or brake servo should be noted, particularly in the case of the latter, as a leaky cylinder can contaminate the servo, and the pedal box and steering column need removing to replace this. While you're looking at it, check the brake fluid cap fastens properly, as the thread on the plastic reservoir can 'round-off,' meaning the cap will tighten, before 'clicking' and then releasing again.

Brakes

Braking components were sourced from Ford's Sierra, initially with 400 models using a smaller diameter disc to the larger engine versions, after which all models were upgraded to the larger setup from 1996/7 onwards. They're a simple system but as with all floating calliper systems, check the faces of the discs for scoring or uneven wear, as this could indicate seized or worn slider pins, as well as potential piston problems. The inner face of the rear discs are particularly sensitive.

The brake fluid should be renewed every few years, but many cars miss out on this, and as a result suffer from corrosion in the bores due to a high moisture concentration (the clutch even more so).

Some owners fit bigger brakes, the execution and effectiveness of which can vary from car to car. These are worth having inspected, post-purchase, to make sure the conversion has been completed correctly.

Fuel lines and hose(s)

From the factory, these cars were equipped with copper lines and rubber hoses. Though the hose was normally a quality product, this is now past its useful life, and there's a strong chance it needs replacing, if it hasn't been already.

There's also another potential issue, in the form of poor quality replacement rubber fuel hose. Indeed, I've seen cars where the owners (very sensibly) opted to have their fuel hose renewed as a matter of course, only to find the product it was replaced with begins to perish within 18-24 months.

This is a big issue that is affecting the entire classic car collective. The most likely areas to suffer are:
• Under the bonnet – both the 8mm (5/16) supply and return lines emerge from the right-hand rear corner of the engine bay (alongside the brake and clutch pipes), and cross over the top of the rocker cover into the fuel rail. The hoses create a sharp radius while doing this, and coupled with the heat from the exhaust manifold below, this is both the most important area to check, and the most likely to exhibit

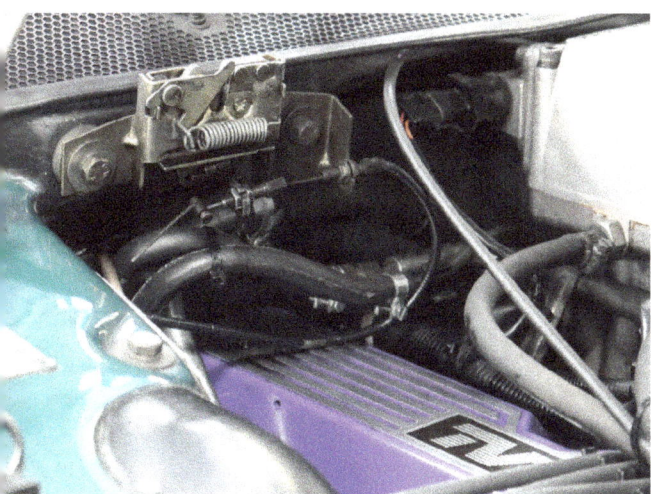

Check the fuel hoses at the top right of the engine bay for signs of fractures or perishing. Note the purple rocker covers, fitted to all 500 models.

This short stretch of hose is behind the left rear wheel, at the back of the wishbone. If it looks as bad as this one, there's a chance the section before it is just as bad, and removal of the fuel tank will be necessary to replace it.

symptoms of failure.
• At the fuel pump – located behind the left-hand rear wheel on the lower chassis rail, just obscured by the lower wishbone. There are two short sections of 13mm diameter hose before the pump, through which the supply passes from the tank. Barely visible is a short piece on the spigot of the tank, obscured by the body. This then passes into a copper 'bridge' pipe, before another short piece of 13mm hose connects this to the pump. The earliest cars didn't use the copper bridge pipe, and in such cases a single length of rubber hose was used; If this is the case, check it's not fouling the lower wishbone. Check all related hoses for dampness; signs of perishing, or whether it feels unnaturally soft under compression (a sign the fuel has penetrated the rubber). These sections aren't pressurised, but renewal will involve the draining and possible removal of the fuel tank.

• At the fuel filter – this will be even trickier to spot, so follow the 8mm high pressure hose, which exits the pump and climbs up the side of the chassis towards the fuel filter. This is located just above the nose of the differential, and again is a place where the hoses have to make some tight radius turns to reach the filter. Any signs of perishing here suggest the rest of the circuit under the car needs renewing – budget accordingly.

While you're at the fuel filter, note the condition of it; TVRs service intervals state the filter should renewed as part of a major service, but due to poor access, it's often omitted. Its exclusion could suggest that other, more serious areas of maintenance have been skipped, too.

Lastly, unscrew the fuel cap. The fuel tank is set up to breathe, but a sudden intake or exhale on removal of the cap suggests this system is faulty.

Cooling system

Inspect the rubber hoses for signs of fracturing, perished rubber or evidence of a leak, especially around the hose clips. There are also various metal pipes situated around the engine bay, which can corrode and leak.

Check around the water pump for signs of a failed seal or gasket, and with the engine cold, check the pulley for excess play.

'Pre-serp' engines employed a single alloy coolant swirl pot, bolted

Don't ignore damp patches or evidence of corrosion in a radiator core: they're an expensive item to renew!

to the front of the engine, while later 'serp' engines use a slightly smaller swirl pot mounted on the chassis cross-brace, ahead of the engine, with an additional expansion tank. Check for air bubbles appearing in the coolant while the engine is running, especially on the 450.

The cooling fans should cut in together at full speed between 92-96°C (depending on the fan switch used) and cut-out again around 88°C. If they run continuously, it's an indication that all is not well, and while that could be a simple fix, it could also be a significant problem. On the cruise, it should sit at around 80°C on a 'reasonably' accurate gauge, or around mid-way on the needle, though it's worth pointing out that the coolant temperature gauge often under-reads.

Radiator

Original radiators are a conventional copper core type with a bleed screw on the top right corner. They work well, but the type of antifreeze used can affect the lifespan of the unit. Some more modern coolants can attack the solder in older copper radiator cores, so look for tell-tale signs of coolant leaks and pink stains around the edges of the core. Check that it's been changed on schedule, too: low annual mileage is irrelevant, because, as with brake fluid, it's time, not usage that causes deterioration.

Many cars will have had a lightweight alloy replacement radiator fitted, as the original copper cores are no longer available. Some people champion the original items, so opt to have them refurbished. Neither option is cheap, though the alloy items are generally more costly. Allow x350, and 2-3 hours labour if you suspect it needs renewing.

Idle speed
The stepper motor, as it's commonly referred to, is an idle bypass valve. If the revs are fluctuating at idle, it may be sticking, which is common after periods where the car isn't used. It could also be leaky vacuum hoses, or even the plenum chamber or intake manifold.

Engine
For the most part, the Rover V8 is a tough, well-proven engine. The 4.0 and 4.3 versions could probably be considered the least likely to cause you trouble, however, there are some areas to check, both during inspection, and on the road.

Oil leaks (all)
It's likely the sump will be oily, though the source of it might be more than just its gasket. The timing cover of the front of the engine can leak, culminating below the crankshaft pulley, and a rear main crankshaft oil seal would require gearbox removal to rectify (though even oil from a leaky sump will collect around here during use). Rocker cover gaskets frequently leak, though they're simple to change. Many people joke that the time to start worrying about a Rover V8, is when the oil leaks suddenly stop!

Hint: If any leaks around the rear of the sump are red, it's almost certainly coming from the transmission, as the specified lubricant is ATF.

Camshaft wear (all)
The camshaft profile contains sixteen lobes (the cross-section of which are 'egg-shaped'), which control the timing and duration of the inlet and exhaust valves opening. It's driven by a chain from the crankshaft, which rarely gives any trouble, but a common problem on the Rover V8 is the lobes of the camshaft 'rounding off' over time. This reduces the amount the valves can open, thus restricting the engine's breathing ability, primarily at higher revs. It's safe to assume that an original camshaft with over 50,000 miles (approx. 80,000 km) on it stands a chance of being worn out, and any increase in valve clearances caused by these worn lobes are masked by the hydraulic lifters, so the engine won't be uncharacteristically 'tappy'. It likely won't be easily noticeable on the road, either, as below 3000rpm, a worn cam exhibits few symptoms (as the engine doesn't require so much valve lift). In fact, it's been known to improve low-range torque! During hard acceleration above 4500rpm, however, the engine will become breathless (especially felt in higher gears) due to the restriction valves that don't open fully present. There aren't many opportunities to test this on the road, though.

Piston slap (aka 'Death rattle')
Mostly confined to the 500 models, this is a subtle tapping or rattling noise audible on the overrun, whether stationary or on the move. It's a symptom of the special pistons used in the 5.0 variant, which can wear after 40-50k miles, and 'rattle' in

their bores as they travel on a downward stroke. Re-honing the bores and replacing the pistons is the only cure, and a costly one, too. It should be noted that while a car may show symptoms, it's rare for an actual failure to occur.

Excessive pressurisation of cooling system (all)

Normally either head gasket failure, or a dislodged cylinder liner; either way, an expensive fix. Obviously, a cooling system needs to pressurise, but to make sure it's not excessive, start the engine from cold, blip the throttle a few times, turn it off after 40-50 seconds, and immediately remove the coolant pressure cap. If you hear a loud hiss, or lots of bubbles rise as you open the tank, it suggests all is not well.

Porous blocks (450)

This is an issue almost exclusively contained to the 4.6-based P38 Range Rover engines, where poor castings in the cylinder block can lead to the increased risk of a dislodged cylinder liner, and the symptoms listed above. Rover engine specialists, V8 Developments, suggest that the symptoms of affected engines tend to reveal themselves after approx 70k miles.

Corrosion on the face of the mating flange of this exhaust manifold means the gasket has been unable to seal properly, so watch out for heavily corroded manifolds/ headers.

This small barrel section is the pre-cat (note that the welding at each end matches). It generates more heat than the rest of the manifold, and on the nearside a small heatshield should be present to protect the surrounding componentry, but it is often missing, so check for burnt or damaged wiring.

The majority of cars will feature a Y-piece exhaust section containing a large barrel catalytic converter. If this is missing, the car will likely fail the relevant emissions regulations of an annual inspection.

Exhaust (manifolds/headers)

Inspect the manifolds (aka 'headers') which, unlike most Rover V8-engined vehicles, run forwards from the engine, allowing it to be positioned as far back as possible to more evenly distribute weight. These are susceptible to leaks, which can't always be detected at tickover, but can be detected on a test drive by 'clicking' or

A Griffith 'pre-cat' engine bay. Note each branch of the manifolds remain individual up to the Y-piece, where they flow into one section.

'tapping' noises from the engine, relative to throttle load (especially at low engine speeds in higher gears). The most common culprits are the manifold gaskets to the cylinder heads, which get a hard life as many models had cylinder heads with enlarged exhaust ports, as well as exhausts that don't always sit perfectly square to the heads. You should haggle accordingly, as it's labour-intensive enough to be a concern. The manifold faces aren't always completely flat, either, so some cars do 'eat' gaskets – check the history.

Don't assume a detected leak is the gaskets for certain, however. It's been known for the manifolds to fracture in and around the 4-into-1 collector. It could be hard to detect this, so just do your best to look for any signs of cracking, or black sooty stains. If you notice a marked difference between the standard of welding, it's possible the exhaust has already been patched up, and such repairs are normally only a temporary cure.

On applicable models, there are three catalytic converters: In each manifold/ header, there is a 'pre-cat' (not to be confused with the Griffith 'pre-cat'). This is fitted before the main catalyst, and is required to keep emissions down when the car is started from cold. To try and reduce under-bonnet temperatures, it's common for owners to have these removed, either by cutting the manifold open and welding it up again, or breaking up and removing the element from inside, leaving no visual evidence that this has been carried out. The car should still meet the emissions standards, but may require warming up to do so. A negative effect of this process is that the exhaust gases can resonate more in the manifold, which can sometimes give an effect similar to that of a leak.

The manifolds flow into the 'Y-piece,' and it's here that the main catalytic converter lives. It's important to check the car still has this fitted, as it will not pass the UK's MOT test if it's missing (along with the majority of equivalent tests in other countries). If the Y-piece fitted has no 'barrel' (or it does, but there is evidence of welding that differs from the surrounding areas), it may have been removed.

Engine mounts

Not a particularly difficult component to change, but worth checking because failing

Engine mount failure causes the engine to sit too low, which leads to contact between the underside of the exhaust manifolds and the chassis and suspension damper, which in turn leads to failure of those, too!

engine mounts can cause the engine to drop within the chassis, leading to contact between the underside of the exhaust headers the surrounding chassis. This could cause damage to the suspension damper bushes, the chassis coating and the headers themselves, as the weight and movement of the engine combined with the heat generated could lead to fractures.

Exhaust (main system)

Both models use the same basic assemblies, though they're not interchangeable, as the tailpipes on the Chimaera are longer. The system connects to the bottom of the Y-piece, and runs alongside the engine and transmission into a single silencer, which is mounted on a metal plate. It's very difficult to inspect any of this without being directly underneath the car, but thankfully the only likely issue will be perished rubber mounts, which are cheap to buy and simple to fit. Also worth checking is the rear rubber hanger; A relatively lightweight affair, it serves the purpose of supporting the tailpipes. Check there isn't excessive play when moving the tailpipes up and down, because a failed mounting or incorrectly supported exhaust can cause the tailpipes to fracture around the welds where they join the centre silencer.

Aside from the additional or removal of minor bracketry, TVR only really made one alteration to the system throughout production, which was the addition of a flexible length of pipe, situated alongside the gearbox bellhousing. It's susceptible to leaks and can be damaged with repeated contact with the ground, particularly on cars with lower ride heights than normal. Inspect it for tell-tale black stains, to highlight any possible damage.

Many owners have their systems modified by cutting the silencer open, removing the perforated pipes and replacing them with solid ones, creating a straight-through system, which is much louder as a result. These are carried out with varying degrees of success, so look for uneven tailpipes to indicate the system may have distorted during welding, and listen for buzzing sounds, suggesting the exhaust could be fouling the chassis. It's a purely subjective matter as to whether sleeved silencers are a desirable feature or not, but be aware of cars that are advertised with a 'sports exhaust'; In rare cases, it will actually refer to one of the aftermarket stainless items on the market, but in most cases it'll translate simply as the above.

Chassis

The elephant in the room – the chassis – is fabricated from a combination of round and rectangular tubular steel, which forms a rigid 'backbone' all the way from the front to the rear, creating a 'tunnel' in which the entire powertrain is housed. The occupants sit each side of this, while the nose and tail of the body tub attach to it at either end. The unequal length double-wishbones and suspension dampers are mounted to the top and bottom rails of this, too, which is why its integrity is crucial. The outriggers, meanwhile, are made of

The standard exhaust layout of either car. Note the system merges into one pipe before splitting into the two tailpipes, which means each tailpipe is not unique to the corresponding side of the engine. Note also the damage caused to the flexible section near the gearbox, fitted to 450 and 500 models.

round steel tube, and protrude outwards from the lower chassis rails towards the side edges of the body tub; Their primary task is to support the body, though your seatbelts and lower suspension wishbones are also mounted to them, so it's vital that they are sound.

When inspecting for rust, check everywhere you possibly can, but the most likely places to find trouble are:

The outriggers are the first area that springs to mind with these cars when

The corner sections of the outriggers are the first to rot. Not all will be as obvious to the eye as this ...

... though it could be worse: this chassis had a piece of children's play equipment inserted disguised as the outrigger tubing!

mentioning 'chassis' and 'corrosion,' but there's more to be concerned with.

Outriggers

Firstly, a car advertised as having had 'new outriggers' isn't exempt, as you're just as likely to find a car with bodged outriggers as you are good ones, no matter who did the work. Try and ascertain whether the body was removed, or at least lifted in order to carry this out.

Start inspecting by locating the front corners immediately behind the wheelarch (use torch and screwdriver). Look for holes, flaking rust, paint that's been applied over rust, and lumpy/bumpy welding. The position of the body restricts your access to get in there closely, but poke any area in the corner as best you can. Follow the tube inwards towards the rectangular lower chassis rails, and inspect the diagonal brace that comes down and meets the outrigger in the wheelarch. The rearmost corners are obscured by the seatbelt mounting tabs too; these need inspecting closely for signs of wastage of the metal, or heavy rusting. A recent MOT pass means little on these cars, as the areas that fail are largely hidden.

A simple rule of thumb: however bad it looks on the parts you can see, it's two or three times worse on the parts you can't.

View from the left-hand front wheelarch. This is about all you can see of the outriggers here. Note the only welds are at the ends of the tubing, with nothing in the centre; anything more suggests repairs have been carried out. Note also the build-up of road dirt and debris flicked up by the wheels. This can hide holes in the tubing, so be prepared to ask the seller if you can clear it out.

The right-hand rear outrigger corner, this time viewed from underneath. With the body lifted away from the chassis, we can see evidence of a previous owner's efforts to preserve the chassis with white paint, but this guarantees nothing, as there are still rusted sections that are out of reach.

Lower rails

The outriggers meet the rectangular lower chassis rails at the front, centre & rear sections, and are gusseted with 3mm plate steel, welded both top and bottom. This is a common area to find corrosion or holes, especially above the plate on the upper welds on cars with the white chassis. Issues with the lower rail tend to form initially on the left-hand side, where the front outrigger meets it. This is likely because the carbon canister vent hose is attached here, and can trap moisture and debris.

In an ideal world, your car's chassis will look like this. The owner's chosen colour scheme on this 500 model is likely a 'love or hate' situation, but it certainly makes the design of the chassis stand out.

You really need to make sure the outriggers are strong and solid; in this instance, the outriggers were so weak the body was holding them together, and when it was removed, they fell off!

Back at the left-hand front lower arch, this time looking deeper towards the lower chassis rails. These rectangular sections are critical to the structural integrity of the chassis, as they tend to rot here first. Note the cable-ties – these hold a fuel breather hose, and the rust normally begins around it. As with the rest of the chassis, it's the areas you can't easily see that you need to closely inspect!

Same corner again, this time with the body removed. Now we can see the round upper chassis rails. The heat from the exhausts has damaged the powdercoating, allowing rust to form, and in this case, spread quite dramatically. Note the lower rectangular rail, mentioned above; we can see a hole in it, roughly in line with where that rubber fuel breather hose runs. These areas are difficult to inspect with the car in one piece, though it is possible using a combination of mirrors and torches!

Surface rust needs to be taken seriously. This is the underside of an upper rail on a chassis which has been grit-blasted to remove all traces of corrosion. Prior to this, there were no holes here, only surface rust. Post-blasting, we discover this, and that means that despite only having 'surface rust,' the chassis was weakened.

Upper rails

The tubular upper chassis rails also often fail to escape the clutches of corrosion. Primarily concerning the areas around the front upper wishbones, and the sections directly below the exhaust headers (where the heat generated can damage the original powder coating), the surface can corrode heavily on this structural section.

Wishbones

Obviously, wishbones are not a part of the chassis, but you may as well

Wishbones are safety-critical, though, thankfully, rectification isn't the potential trip-hazard the chassis might be. They're currently available off the shelf, but beware of potential mounting costs if the car has a number of them that look like this! Remember, with wishbone replacement comes the necessity of suspension bush renewal, and the potential headache of seized fixings or swivel joints. Costs can snowball!

regard them as such if they're rusted. There are eight all-round, with only the lower rears being tubular. The remaining arms are made of pressed and folded, gusseted and welded. Check them inside and out for corrosion. On the lower rear arms, the anti-roll bar mounting plate gets a tough life, and any corrosion here normally results in a fracture, so if it's been repaired, check it's a good one.

The test drive

All Chimaeras or Griffiths will differ behind the wheel, but you'll have no frame of reference unless you drive lots of them, so concern yourself with whether or not you like the one you're in, even if you're only buying it as a project; the more you drive it, the more you'll discover what's in need of repair.

There's little point me trying to describe to you exactly how you should interpret the car on the move, because they're a bit of an assault on the senses, and you'd need a long time behind the wheel to systematically go through any list of areas I scribble down. So, concentrate on the basics; is it tracking straight, or pulling to one side? What about under braking, or hard acceleration? You're likely to find the unassisted steering and other controls slightly heavy, unless you're used to older cars, but these aren't difficult cars to master on the road.

A well-sorted car will feel composed, but a badly-sorted one can feel very unsettled over rough roads.

Try driving steady at 30mph in 5th gear - some cars can't manage it smoothly, suggesting further issues. 'Shunting' is a common issue, though often a misdescribed one, too. In some cases, the cars do indeed 'shunt,' whereby even with the throttle held steady, the engine surges back and forth resulting in jerky

Try to include some more challenging routes in your test drive to put the car through its paces, like this road in Basildon, Essex ... or not!
(Courtesy www.pub2pubadventures.com)

progress. This can be the result of numerous causes, but some people confuse shunting with how an undiluted, lightweight, V8 RWD sports car goes about its business; uncouthly!

While the car is rolling – regardless of gear or throttle input - it should 'fast idle' at around 1100-1200rpm up until the car becomes stationary, when it should settle to normal idle (850-900rpm). This is a buffer mapped into the ECU, which smoothes out any less-than-sympathetic throttle inputs. If this mode isn't functioning, progress in traffic or at low speed won't be smooth, and you may find the car stalls as you roll up to junctions. The ECU requires a speed signal to achieve this, but in most cases the components, in effect, don't speak the same language. For this reason, TVR wired a control box into the dashboard, which converts the signal for the ECU. If this box, the speedo sender, the speedo itself, or the throttle position sensor fail, the idle mode won't function properly.

Check that there are no flat spots in the rev range under hard acceleration, and that it will readily administer a kick to your spleen from any engine speed! All models should pull hard up to around 5500rpm. Revving this fast is pointless day to day, but you need to make sure it doesn't become breathless at 4000-4500rpm. Check also for ticking or tapping in higher gears at lower speeds, which could be those pesky exhaust manifolds.

You might detect noises from the rear suspension, but the best cars are void of rattles or clunks. A TVR that feels as tightly screwed together as a modern car is a rare thing. Remember to drive it with the roof on, too, otherwise the sound of a problem might be drowned out by wind and a noisy exhaust.

Try coming on and off the power sharply, listening for excessive drivetrain backlash, and check there is no grinding when changing into second and third gear, and that the boxes are relatively quiet in neutral at tickover with your foot off the clutch; a small amount of noise is acceptable, but if you suspect it's louder than it should be, rest your foot on the clutch pedal: if it disappears immediately, the release bearing is the probably cause. It it remains, depress the pedal further: if the noise fades more gradually, it's likely the gearbox itself. Neither are a cheap

If, during the test drive, you find yourself making this face, it's likely an indication that you've either found a bad car, or a really, really good one!
(Courtesy G Leach/T Matthews)

repair, but the latter is considerably more costly. The biting point should be smooth, with no evidence of clutch judder (shuddering as the clutch disengages).

As the clutch friction plate wears, the sprung fingers on the cover plate protrude further out, which moves the bite point further up the pedal. If the bite point feels high during the test drive, select 4th gear at a low speed (no more than 35mph) and, with your foot resting (NOT pressing) on the clutch pedal, floor the throttle sharply (when safe to do so) for a few seconds to check for signs of clutch slippage; If the revs suddenly rise too quickly in relation to the car's road speed - even if only briefly - the clutch is slipping. A clutch typically lasts around 50-70k miles on the larger engine variants, while a sympathetically-driven 400 can keep going until 80-100k miles. Check the paperwork for evidence it's been changed.

Hint: You may find that on T-5 equipped cars, reverse doesn't select without complaint. The smoothest way to select reverse in such circumstances, is to first select 5th gear, then move directly down to reverse.

All models feature a limited-slip differential , though you won't feel the effects of this unless you begin driving in a manner that will upset the vendor. Go to a car park and try manoeuvring on full lock in both directions to listen for 'thumping' or clicking noises, though. A tired diff is at its noisiest when under load in a high gear. Don't expect a silent diff (there's no real soundproofing, and it's just behind you), but excessive whining may point to a problem.

Evaluation procedure
Add up the total points.
Score: 140 = excellent; 105 = good; 70 = average; 35 = poor.
Cars scoring over 98 will be completely usable and will require only maintenance and care to preserve condition.
Cars scoring between 35 and 71 will require some serious work (at much the same cost regardless of score).
Cars scoring between 72 and 97 will require very careful assessment of the necessary repair/restoration costs in order to arrive at a realistic value.

10 Auctions

– sold! Another way to buy your dream

Auction pros & cons

Pros: Prices will usually be lower than those of dealers or private sellers and you might grab a bargain on the day. Auctioneers have usually established clear title with the seller. At the venue you can usually examine documentation relating to the vehicle.
Cons: You have to rely on a sketchy catalogue description of condition and history. The opportunity to inspect is limited and you cannot drive the car. Auction cars are often a little below par and may require some work. It's easy to overbid. There will usually be a 'buyer's premium' to pay in addition to the auction hammer price.

Which auction?

Auctions by established auctioneers are advertised in car magazines and on the auction houses' websites. A catalogue, or a simple printed list of the lots for auctions might only be available a day or two ahead, though often lots are listed and pictured on auctioneers' websites much earlier. Contact the auction company to ask if previous auction selling prices are available as this is useful information (details of past sales are often available on websites).

Catalogue, entry fee and payment details

When you purchase the catalogue of the vehicles in the auction, it often acts as a ticket allowing two people to attend the viewing days and the auction. Catalogue details tend to be comparatively brief, but will include information such as 'one owner from new, low mileage, full service history,' etc. It will also usually show a guide price to give you some idea of what to expect to pay and will tell you what is charged as the buyer's premium. The catalogue will also contain details of acceptable forms of payment. At the fall of the hammer an immediate deposit is usually required, the balance payable within 24 hours. If the plan is to pay by cash there may be a cash limit. Some auctions will accept payment by credit or debit cards, but may incur an extra charge. A bank draft or bank transfer will have to be arranged in advance with your own bank as well as with the auction house. No car will be released before all payments are cleared. If delays occur in payment transfers then storage costs can accrue.

Buyer's premium

A buyer's premium will be added to the hammer price: *don't* forget this in your calculations. It is not usual for there to be a further state tax or local tax on the purchase price and/or on the buyer's premium.

Viewing

In some instances it's possible to view on the day, or days before, as well as in the hours prior to, the auction. There are auction officials available who are willing to help out by opening engine and luggage compartments and allow you to inspect the interior. While the officials may start the engine for you, a test drive is out of the question. Crawling under and around the car as much as you want is permitted, but you can't suggest that the car you are interested in be jacked up, or attempt to do the job yourself. You can also ask to see any documentation available.

Bidding

Before you take part in the auction, *decide your maximum bid – and stick to it!*

It may take a while for the auctioneer to reach the lot you are interested in, so use that time to observe how other bidders behave. When it's the turn of your car, attract the auctioneer's attention and make an early bid. The auctioneer will then look to you for a reaction every time another bid is made, usually the bids will be in fixed increments until the bidding slows, when smaller increments will often be accepted before the hammer falls. If you want to withdraw from the bidding, make sure the auctioneer understands your intentions - a vigorous shake of the head when he or she looks to you for the next bid should do the trick!

Assuming that you are the successful bidder, the auctioneer will note your card or paddle number, and from that moment on, you will be responsible for the vehicle.

If the car is unsold, either because it failed to reach the reserve or because there was little interest, it may be possible to negotiate with the owner, via the auctioneers, after the sale is over.

Successful bid

There are two more items to think about. How to get the car home, and insurance. If you can't drive the car, your own or a hired trailer is one way, another is to have the vehicle shipped using the facilities of a local company. The auction house will also have details of companies specialising in the transfer of cars.

Insurance for immediate cover can usually be purchased on site, but it may be more cost-effective to make arrangements with your own insurance company in advance, and then call to confirm the full details.

eBay & other online auctions?

eBay and other online auctions could land you a car at a bargain price, though you'd be foolhardy to bid without examining the car first, something most vendors encourage. Be prepared to be outbid in the last few moments of the auction. Remember, your bid is binding and that it will be very, very difficult to get restitution in the case of a crooked vendor fleecing you – *caveat emptor!*

Be aware that some cars offered for sale in online auctions are 'ghost' cars. *Don't* part with *any* cash without being sure that the vehicle does actually exist and is as described (usually pre-bidding inspection is possible).

Auctioneers

Barrett-Jackson www.barrett-jackson.com/ **Bonhams** www.bonhams.com/ **British Car Auctions (BCA)** www.bca-europe.com or www.british-car-auctions. co.uk/ **Christies** www.christies.com/ **Coys** www.coys.co.uk/ **eBay** www.eBay. com/ **H&H** www.classic-auctions.co.uk/ **RM** www.rmauctions.com/ **Shannons** www.shannons.com.au/ **Silver** www.silverauctions.com

11 Paperwork
– correct documentation is essential!

The paper trail
Classic, collector and prestige cars usually come with a large portfolio of paperwork accumulated and passed on by a succession of proud owners. This documentation represents the real history of the car and from it can be deduced the level of care the car has received, how much it's been used, which specialists have worked on it, and the dates of major repairs and restorations. All of this information will be priceless to you as the new owner, so be very wary of cars with little paperwork to support their claimed history.

Registration documents
All countries/states have some form of registration for private vehicles whether its like the American 'pink slip' system or the British 'log book' system.

It is essential to check that the registration document is genuine, that it relates to the car in question, and that all the vehicle's details are correctly recorded, including chassis/VIN and engine numbers (if these are shown).

In the UK, registered keeper transfers can now be processed online, meaning this can be completed at point of sale.

Previous ownership records
Due to the introduction of important new legislation on data protection, it is no longer possible to acquire, from the British DVLA, a list of previous owners of a car you own, or are intending to purchase. This scenario will also apply to dealerships and other specialists, from who you may wish to make contact and acquire information on previous ownership and work carried out.

Roadworthiness certificate
Most country/state administrations require that vehicles are regularly tested to prove that they are roadworthy. In the UK that test (the MOT) is carried out at approved testing stations, for a fee. In the USA the requirement varies, but most states insist on an emissions test every two years as a minimum, while the police are charged with pulling over unsafe-looking vehicles.

In the UK the test is required on an annual basis once a vehicle becomes three years old. Of particular relevance for older cars is that the certificate issued includes the mileage reading recorded at the test date and, therefore, becomes an independent record of that car's history. It's desirable to have a collection of previous test certificates within the paperwork, though tests carried out in England, Scotland, and Wales since 2005 have also been logged on an electronic database, which can be accessed online at https://www.gov.uk/check-mot-history. Without an MOT the vehicle should be trailered to its new home, unless you insist that a valid MOT is part of the deal. (Not such a bad idea, this, as at least you will know the car was roadworthy on the day it was tested and you don't need to wait for the old certificate to expire before having the test done.) If the seller is reluctant to submit the car for testing, there could be a serious reason why; a current certificate adds value to the sale price, so if the seller is confident it would pass another, they'd likely have already done it.

Road licence

The administration of every country/state charges some kind of tax for the use of its road system, the actual form of the 'road licence' and how it is displayed, varying enormously from country to country, and state to state.

Whatever the form of the 'road licence' it must relate to the vehicle carrying it and must be present and valid if the car is to be driven legally on the public highway.

In the UK if a car is untaxed because it has not been used for a period of time, the owner has to inform the licencing authorities by declaring the car SORN. This stands for Statutory Off Road Notification and it's used to tell the DVLA that your car isn't parked or being used on public roads.

It's worth noting that sellers in the UK are no longer permitted to transfer any remaining months of tax to a new owner. This means you cannot legally drive the car away from the sale until you tax it, and you cannot tax it until you buy it! You may invalidate your insurance by not taxing it, and not only are you liable to be fined for not having tax, but if you're involved in an accident or have your car stolen you may be fined for not having insurance and even face a criminal conviction.

Because you need to tax the car before you drive it, you need the new keeper section of the V5C, which will allow you to tax the car immediately online, over the phone, or at a Post Office.

Valuation certificate

It's possible that the vendor will have a recent valuation certificate, or letter signed by a recognised expert stating how much he or she believes the particular car to be worth (such documents, together with photos, are sometimes required to obtain 'agreed value' insurance). Generally such documents should act only as confirmation of your own assessment of the car rather than a guarantee of value as the expert has probably not seen the car in the flesh. The easiest way to find out how to obtain a formal valuation is to contact the TVR Car Club (or overseas equivalent).

Service history

It's easy to cloud your own judgement by assuming that for a car that could be around 25 years old, that service history is of little consequence, but it's as much about provenance as it is maintenance. Try to obtain as much service history and other paperwork pertaining to the car as you can. Naturally, dealer stamps, or specialist garage receipts score most points in the value stakes, and rare cases you may be lucky enough to uncover gems such as the original bill of sale, handbook, parts invoices and repair bills, adding to the story and the character of the car. Even a brochure correct to the year of the car's manufacture is a useful document and something that you could well have to search hard to locate in future years. The most pertinent aspect, when it comes to paperwork, is the proof that something has been carried out. Discovering that Car 1 (a 75,000-mile Chimaera 500, for example) had a commonly worn part (eg camshaft) renewed about 10,000 miles previously should save you the cost of having a new one installed (⬤x1000-⬤x1500), which a 75,000 version of that car will likely need. Therefore, Car 1 is effectively offering a discount to that amount over an identically-priced Car 2 that hasn't received the same work. And you didn't even need to haggle!

If the seller claims to have carried out regular servicing, ask what work was completed, when, and seek some evidence of it being carried out. Your assessment of the car's overall condition should tell you whether the seller's claims are genuine,

Photographs are an important part of paperwork for restored cars ...

... they should help you gauge the thoroughness and attention to detail of the work.

and remember: many people incorrectly assume that 'servicing' equates to an oil and filter change. This is not the case with any car, let alone a Griffith or Chimaera.

A sign of a looked-after car is a privately-advertised car being sold by a member of a TVR Car Club or owner's group (especially if they're replacing it with another model of the same marque) as nobody would knowingly sell a poor car when there's a chance you'll meet each other again. Service history plays a significant part in a car's value, as the story of how the car arrived at where it is today is a strong selling tool. Evidence that the car has been mechanically cared for over the years is telling, because if somebody agonised looking after the paperwork and written history of the car, the odds are they took the time to look after the car itself too.

Restoration photographs
If the seller claims that the car has received specialist repair or attention, such as a body-off chassis restoration, or a full respray or retrim, ask to see the pictures, if they aren't enthusiastically waving them in front of you already.

12 What's it worth?
– let your head rule your heart

The specification clearly plays a major role (eg a Chimaera 500 is worth more than a 400), and to some extent the year of manufacture and mileage, with later, lower mileage cars often considered more desirable.

Figuring out what kind of future costs might be incurred is important, however. The chassis is the most significant influence on the value of a chosen model, simply because it's the most costly thing to put right. There are three categories your chosen car's chassis could fall under:

• Original: it's possible for a car to have an original, sound chassis, though the majority will have some patches of surface rust in various areas. Expect to find a few scattered areas where sections of the original powdercoating have flaked off, normally around welds or along sharp edges, such as suspension eyelets. This is to be expected, whereas larger areas of corrosion along chassis rails and members could develop into significant problems. Beware any chassis that is caked in black underseal, too: it's very good at hiding rust!

• Repaired with body-on: the cheapest method of outrigger replacement is to raise the body just enough to cut them off, weld on new ones and hand-paint them. It's possible to carry out a good repair in this manner, but remember it's not just the outriggers that rust. The other issue is that some cars will have had the outriggers replaced without the body being raised. The repair is likely to be compromised in terms of chassis strength and corrosion resistance, as there isn't the access required to weld the tubes fully on, unless you cut out sections of the body tub, but even that has mixed results. I would prefer a car with reasonably solid original outriggers over those that have been replaced without lifting the body.

This factory-original silver chassis is in sound condition. The grease and muck dispersed by the engine, transmission, universal joints and such can actually provide some decent rust prevention qualities.

This car is having the outriggers renewed by means of a 'body-lift.' The access is sufficient so that a comprehensive repair can be made. The only drawback of this is that it only concerns the outriggers and lower rails; the rest of the chassis may need attention, too.

Lifting the body is a time-consuming process, and some owners like to cut costs (and corners) by having the outriggers replaced with the body in-situ. Alarm bells should ring here, because although not every repair is necessarily poor, the majority of them look something like this, once you've stripped it back. Note the missed welds, and the hole that has appeared after the grit blast, meaning all that work still didn't fix the problem.

• Restored with body-off: cars that have had body-off chassis refurbishments are the best place to put your money, without doubt, because the chassis should have been examined closely, repaired and then fully coated. Invariably, people have to attend to more than just the chassis, and many mechanical components are renewed at the same time. The cost to have a chassis overhauled professionally is rarely fully recovered in the future value of the car, so it's better value to buy one that has been overhauled already. Questions to ask include: who carried out the refurb? What chassis coating was used? (Some are much better than others.) If the

Is this beautiful Griffith 500 in excellent, good or average condition? There's no right or wrong here; it's simply down to your expectations. One piece of advice I will offer is to not get bogged down in every little body imperfection; these are driver's cars, and, in the process of being used properly, they pick up imperfections. Prioritise your concerns.

refurbishment was of good quality, expect to pay a 30-50 per cent premium for a car that has been subject to a body-off restoration.

The paintwork and interior are more subjective. What one person considers show-worthy, another considers atrocious. Only you know what you're happy with, or what you're willing to spend further funds on. Get some rough quotes to complete any work you're not happy with, and factor this in your negotiations.

Modifications

Many owners often add their own little touches and 'upgrades,' and these bear less impact on the residuals than with many other marques. Certain modifications could be considered desirable, too.

This '93 Griffith 400 is original in nearly every way ... except the rather beautiful equal-length tubular exhaust manifold setup. Who said aftermarket parts had to be a negative?

Of course, if a Chimaera 500 doesn't have enough grunt for your tastes, you could bolt a big turbo onto the end of the manifolds like Barrie Piper has done to his 1998 model. Is 527bhp enough for you?

Another way of joining the high-BHP club is to fit one of GM's 'LS' V8 engines, as fitted to Chevrolet Corvettes and Vauxhall/Holden Monaros, among (many) others. Tread carefully as, in some instances, the chassis may have been structurally modified, which may invalidate the type approval of the model, resulting in the possibility that the car might need to go through a tough inspection such as the IVA (Individual Vehicle Approval), and re-registration (likely a 'Q' prefix in the UK). (Courtesy J Mott)

Modifications needn't be restricted to the mechanical; this Chimaera has received the later Cerbera-style nose. Whether this is a good or bad thing is purely subjective, but inspect the quality of the conversion as there are a number of poor quality examples, with uneven lines and weak spots leading to fracturing, particularly around the wheelarch area. (Courtesy J Mott)

Such modifications may include:
- 500-spec 260mm/273mm larger brake conversion to early 400/430 models.
- Upgraded camshaft (eg MC1 or 'Stealth' fast road specification by V8D Developments).
- Induction modifications, such as smooth-bore intake pipe.
- Alloy radiator/silicone coolant hoses.
- Quality aftermarket exhausts (eg ACT 'twin cherry-bomb' system) or upgraded manifold setup.
- Polyurethane suspension and differential bushes (beware cheaper versions, however).

If a modification is easily reversible, then it shouldn't negatively affect the value of the car, but if it's effectively an irreversible modification, such as an engine conversion, then it is simply down to the buyer's own tastes as to how the value is affected. Generally, the car will be less desirable.

Body modifications normally have a negative impact on the value of a car, as does the removal of hard-to-find parts, such as original wheels or interiors, because a heavily modified car has a narrower potential market than an original car.

If you're looking at any of these alterations in a positive light, remember that other buyers may not, and one day you may be trying to sell the car to them! Is the modification in question reversible? That's the key. (Courtesy J Mott)

13 Do you really want to restore?
– it'll take longer and cost more than you think

If you're considering a project car due to budget, but aren't mechanically minded, proceed with caution. If a TVR is a must, there are others which can fulfill at least some of the briefs achieved by either car, at a lower cost. You don't want your dream car to become a nightmare.

If the challenge of rescuing a car that has fallen on hard times and giving it a new lease of life is one you relish, then either car could be a good proposition for you. What bears a substantial impact on how financially viable restoring either car is, is whether you're doing the work yourself, as, unless funding is of no concern, these cars can cost at least their market value (or more) to have restored professionally. Though fairly simple cars, they're labour-intensive, but if you're skilled and enjoy the process, that adds to the fun. The parts supply is good, and the ownership community is a friendly and enthusiastic one. Provided you buy shrewdly, you could end up with a car equal to some of the best on the market,

If you pick up a project, be prepared for scenes like this. This particular car had been bodged with fibreglass wrapped over the remains of the outrigger tubing, and black sealant used to replicate welds, before it was smothered in thick black underseal.

This Chimaera is known as 'Rob.' It's been rolled, written-off, repaired, badly painted, the mileage is incorrect, there's no history, and it was covered in tacky modifications. It's exactly the sort of car *not* to buy. That's why we (Southways Automotive) did in 2012! It's currently being restored, but we could have bought a pristine car by now for the same cost.

potentially for less outlay. You do need to be honest with yourself about your abilities, however, because a badly restored car will be worth less than an original one.

Buying one of these cars purely with the intention of 'trading up,' is very risky. Unless you can carry out every element of the restoration yourself, you're unlikely to see a profit unless the car was originally priced significantly below market value.

If you do not possess technical ability; strong attention to detail and a good finish, then I would recommend simply buying the best you can afford to

Sometimes, you don't realise what you're getting into. This Chimaera appears solid, and passed the last MOT. But scrape back years of underseal, and what might be lurking underneath?

start with, and maintaining the condition. It's the safest place to be, and unless you harbour an unrelenting urge to get your hands dirty, then it's where the sensible money goes. There will be plenty to keep you occupied in the meantime.

Nearly all of these cars will need at least some level of restoration eventually, so you should keep one eye on the future. There are many adverts that mention "some slight chassis surface rust, but solid" like it's not a bad thing. Of course, gaping holes with flaky edges are much worse, but they all started as surface corrosion, too. Turning down a car you really like because it had a hole in the outrigger would be a tough call, but to then purchase a car which had 'just some surface rust' only puts you in the same position later on: rust doesn't go away – it's a ticking time-bomb, and you don't want to be there when it goes off.

14 Paint problems

– bad complexion, including dimples, pimples and bubbles

Paint faults generally occur due to lack of protection/maintenance, or to poor preparation prior to a respray or touch-up. Some of the following conditions may be present in the car you're looking at:

Orange peel

This appears as an uneven paint surface, similar to the appearance of the skin of an orange. It's caused by the failure of atomized paint droplets to flow into each other when they hit the surface. It's sometimes possible to rub out the effect with proprietary paint cutting/rubbing compound, or very fine grades of abrasive paper. A respray may be necessary in severe cases. Consult a bodywork repairer/paint shop for advice on the particular car.

Cracking

Severe cases are likely to have been caused by too heavy an application of paint (or filler beneath the paint). Also, insufficient stirring of the paint before application can lead to the components being improperly mixed, and cracking can result. Incompatibility with the paint already on the panel can have a similar effect. To rectify the problem, it's necessary to rub down to a smooth, sound finish before respraying the problem area.

Crazing

Sometimes the paint takes on a crazed rather than cracked appearance, when the problems mentioned under 'Cracking' are present. This problem can also be caused by a reaction between the underlying surface and the paint. Removing the paint and respraying the problem area is usually the only solution.

Orange peel.

Cracking and crazing.

Micro blistering.

Micro blistering

Usually the result of an economy respray, where inadequate heating has allowed moisture to settle on the car before spraying. Consult a paint specialist, but usually damaged paint will have to be removed before partial or full respraying. Can also be caused by car covers that don't 'breathe.'

Fading

Some colours, especially reds, are prone to fading if subjected to strong sunlight for long periods, without the benefit of polish protection. Sometimes proprietary paint restorers, and/or paint cutting/ rubbing compounds, will retrieve the situation. Often a respray is the only real solution.

Peeling

Often a problem with metallic paintwork, when the sealing lacquer becomes damaged and begins to peel off. Poorly applied paint may also peel. The remedy is to strip and start again.

Dimples

Dimples in the paintwork are caused by the residue of polish (particularly silicone types) not being removed properly before respraying. Paint removal and repainting is the only solution.

GRP & gel-coat cracking

The fibreglass bodywork of a TVR won't dent like a metal body, but impacts can cause cracks and splits instead. While fibreglass is versatile enough to allow a level of repair simply not possible with a metal body, it's a process that needs experience and skill to complete. The body itself features what is known as a gel-coat finish, which is laid-up as part of the laminating process and provides a smooth, hard finish over the rough fibres of the GRP, which the paint is then applied to.

Inspect it closely for cracks though, because although many of them will be no more noticeable than a human-hair laying on the surface, repair of the gel-coat is not straightforward. You also have to remember that crazing or cracking on a GRP body can worsen over time, even with a simple change of outdoor temperature.

GRP/gel-coat cracking.

– just like their owners, TVRs need exercise!

These cars dislike idleness as much as any other car. And, while some vehicles will have lived a life of pampered luxury in a dehumidified garage, many won't.

While the usual checks for any modern classic will apply, there are some specific areas that you need to pay attention to:

• The roof/rear screen needs to be flexible, as it's contorted and compressed when the roof is collapsed. Long periods of exposure to sunlight will harden a rear screen, and it could fracture after a few attempts. The fabric can also lose adhesion to the roof framework, and in some cases shrink to a point when a retrim is required.

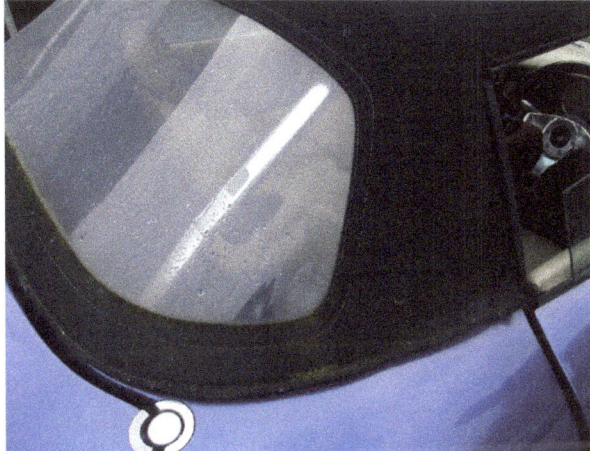

Failing rear screens are commonplace. Inspect the stitching around the edge, and the screen itself for rips and tears all over. Some are more sensitive to UV rays than others, and some owners aren't sympathetic enough when lowering the roof, leading to problems.

• Rubber components are particularly susceptible to problems after periods of disuse. This could include coolant hoses, vacuum hoses, and all suspension and drivetrain mounts/bushes. Also vulnerable are the rubber gaskets and seals on the engine, gearbox, differential and power steering system (if fitted). The fuel lines are also worth checking closely, because all examples are fuel-injected, and therefore any leaks on the supply side will be under pressure. Along with the coolant hoses, inspect the radiator closely for any signs of leaks or heavy corrosion.

• The brake callipers are all of the floating variety. That means, that along with potentially seized pistons, you also run the risk of seized slider pins. A single calliper won't break the bank, but if all four need sorting, along with pipework and flexi-hoses, the costs could escalate quickly.

• If the car hasn't turned a wheel for a significant length of time, the brake disc surfaces will likely be corroded all over, though the portion of the disc concealed by the brake pad on each wheel will corrode to a lesser degree. This effectively creates a 'swelling' on the disc, which can lead to fluctuating brake readings come MOT-time. Brake pads and discs all-round can add up.

• Corroded electrical contacts can cause heaps of trouble. Many of the connectors across the range also use a rubber seal to keep them safe from damp, and if these are missing (as they frequently are) damp could form inside, causing corrosion that can heat up due to resistance and melt the connector body itself.

• Fuel injectors can stick, either from internal corrosion, or by fragments of debris that have clogged up in the circuit. Having all eight injectors removed and refurbished is your remedy.

• Interior materials tended to vary in their quality from the factory, and some cars will have deteriorated worse than others. Don't dismiss a tired interior – the cost to put one right could equate to the difference between the car you bought, and another one you wanted more, but thought you couldn't afford.

• Any evidence of a sticky clutch shouldn't be ignored. What might simply be passed off as something that 'just needs freeing off,' may result in the clutch needing to be changed, and, as mentioned previously, it's an engine out job on earlier cars running the Rover gearbox. The flywheel will likely need refacing too, so although it's not a reason to walk away, consider the added costs and hassle involved. Also consider that though the clutch hydraulics may be functioning happily now, perished or tired rubber will likely lead to a failed seal later down the line, though at least these are more simple fixes.

• Pay close attention to the tyres. Periods of long-standing can lead to flat spots and misshapen rubber, which in turn can lead to vibrations, reduced grip and, in extreme cases, tyre failure. Check the rubber is not hard, and that the sidewalls are free from cracking.

• Paintwork can suffer, especially on cars that have been sitting outside, exposed to the elements, and, of course, the chassis can still rust, even in garages.

The car will be full of clues if it's been living a tough life, like here under the bootlid.

16 The Community

– key people, organisations and companies in the TVR world

Clubs
- UK: TVR Car Club – 01952 822126 / www.tvr-car-club.co.uk
- Belgium: www.tvrcarclub.be
- France: www.tvrcarclub-france.net
- Germany: www.tvrcarclub.de/
- Italy: www.tvrcarclubitalia.com/
- Japan: www.tvrccj.net/
- Netherlands: www.tvrcarclub.nl/
- North America (incl Canada): www.tvrccna.org
- Sweden: http://www.tvrcc.se

You won't be short of social events to attend in these cars. (Courtesy J Mott)

Sales & Dealerships
- Amore Autos (Gloucestershire): www.amoreautos.co.uk/
- Fernhurst Motor Company (Surrey): 01428 653924 / www.fernhurst-tvr.co.uk/
- James Agger Autosport (Leicestershire): 01509 881516 / www.jamesagger.com/
- Racing Green Cars (Hampshire): 01420 511118 / www.racinggreencars.com/
- TVR MADS (Yorkshire): 01274 551955 / www.tvr-mads.co.uk/

Bodywork
- Central TVR (W. Midlands): 01384 571021 / www.centraltvr.com
- Classic Restore (Hampshire): 023 8061 3612 / www.classicrestore.co.uk/
- Option 1 (Worcestershire): 01527 557111 / www.option1sportscars.co.uk

- SD Autotec (N Yorkshire): 01423 329090 / www.sdautotec.co.uk
- Surface and Design Ltd (Bristol Avenue site, Blackpool): 01253 595800 / www.surfaceanddesign.com

Chassis/Engineering/Mechanical
- Classic World Racing (Worcestershire): 01527 521050 / www.classicworldracing.webmate.me
- Lawfield Engineering (Bristol Avenue site, Blackpool): 07810 018747
- Mat Smith Sports Cars (Norfolk): 01366 386004 / www.matsmithsportscars.com
- Powers Performance (W Midlands): 02476 366177 / www.powersperformance.co.uk
- RT Racing (S Yorkshire): 01142 817507 / www.rtracing.co.uk
- Southways Automotive (Hampshire): 01329 220755 / www.southwaysautomotive.co.uk
- Sportmotive (Staffordshire): 01782 333008 / www.sportmotive.com
- Str8six (Oxfordshire): 01844 352735 / www.str8six.co.uk
- TVRSSW (Somerset): 01823 662555 / www.tvrssw.com
- V8 Developments (Lincolnshire): 01775 750000 / www.v8developments.co.uk/
- X-Works (Lancashire): 01772 937177 / www.xworksservice.co.uk

Interior
- Central TVR (W Midlands): 01384 571021 / www.centraltvr.com
- Dave The Trimmer (Bedfordshire): 01908 585 039 / www.davethetrimmer.com/index.html
- D&C Trim (Bristol Avenue site, Blackpool): 07738 130236 / www.dctrim.co.uk/home.html
- Trim Unique (Lancashire): 07885 990113 / www.trim-unique.co.uk

Parts
- ACT Performance Products: 01342 311790 / www.actproducts.co.uk
- Powers Performance: 024 7636 6177 / www.powersperformance.co.uk
- Racetech Direct: 01491 629219 / www.racetechdirect.co.uk
- RT Racing: 0114 281 7507 / www.rtracing.co.uk

You'll have fun wherever you venture, but on trips such as this one, organised by Fast Track Tours, these cars really come alive. (Courtesy G Leach)

• TVR Parts Ltd (TVR's official parts network): 03333 237877 / www.tvr-parts.com
• V8 Developments: 01775 750000 - http://www.v8developments.co.uk/

Ownership community and social scene
• Facebook groups: 'TVR Chimaera owners & enthusiasts,' 'TVR Griffith owners & enthusiasts,' or simply 'TVR Griffith.'
• Pistonheads forum: www.pistonheads.com/gassing (go to TVR subforum and select Chimaera or Griffith as applicable).
• Griffith 500SE information resource: www.griffith500se.co.uk
• TVRCC UK Chimaera info: www.tvr-car-club.co.uk/tvr-chimaera.html
• TVRCC UK Griffith info: www.tvr-car-club.co.uk/tvr-griffith.html
• Fast Track Tours: www.fasttracktours.co.uk

In times gone by, social gatherings have been organised by owners, predominantly in the UK. The events have gone under the name 'Chimfest' and 'Griff Growl,' though these are semi-occasional rather than annual.

The TVR Car Club organises national events throughout the year, as well as local events on a monthly basis. You're almost guaranteed a place in any Pistonheads meet-up, too.

Fast Track Tours are a UK-based company who specialise in both continental and domestic driving holidays and mini-break packages. Predominantly attended by TVR owners, they provide an opportunity to enjoy some of the best driving roads in Europe with like-minded owners.

TVR owners don't need much encouragement to venture out and meet up in the sunshine! Be warned; if you leave the roof on, you will be judged! (Courtesy J Mott)

17 Vital statistics
– essential data at your fingertips

	Chimaera	Griffith
Years produced	1993-2003	1992-2002
Length	4015mm	3892mm
Width	1865mm	1869mm
Height	1215mm	1205mm
Wheelbase	2286mm	2286mm

	400 models	430 models	450 (Griffith pre-cat)	450 (Chimaera)	500 models
Capacity cc	3947cc	4280cc	4497cc	4546cc	4997cc
Bore x stroke	94 x 71.1mm	94 x 77mm	94 x 81mm	94 x 82mm	94 x 90mm
Max power	240bhp @ 5250rpm	280bhp@ 5500rpm	320bhp @ 5700rpm	285bhp @ 5500rpm	340bhp @ 5500rpm
Max torque	270lb/ft @ 4000rpm	305lb/ft @ 4000rpm	310lb/ft @ 4000rpm	310lb/ft @ 4250rpm	350lb/ft @ 3750rpm
0-60mph (claimed)	5.2s	4.9s	4.2s	4.7s	4.1s
Top speed (approx)	152mph	155mph	160mph	160mph	167mph

Timeline

1990	Griffith prototype unveiled.
1992	Griffith 400 and 430 production cars launched. Silver chassis, pre-serp engine, GKN differential, Rover LT77 gearbox
1993	Chimaera 400 and 430 launched (spec as above). Griffith production paused. Griffith 500 launched. Car features open-grille nose, smoked tail lights, and 'Estoril' alloy wheels.
1994	Chimaera 430 replaced by 400 'HC' option. Rover LT77 gearbox replaced by Borg-Warner T5 on all models.
1995	Serpentine engine replaces pre-serp. Power-assisted steering becomes optional. Chimaera 500 launched. Griffith switchgear updated.

1996	Chimaera receives most notable face-lift, with a Cerbera-style slatted radiator grille replacing the black plastic mesh. Rear bumper becomes painted moulding on rear of car, replacing black rubber insert. Bonnet trailing edge redesigned at scuttle. Chassis switch from silver to white powdercoat on all models.
1997	Chimaera 450 launched. Chimaera switchgear and heater controls updated. All Chimaera chassis and brakes upgraded to 500-spec.
1998	Chimaera rear lamps change from Ford-sourced, to individual lenses inside paint recess in bodywork. Rear number plate moves into recess with conventional lighting, replacing the existing backlit design.
1999	Chimaera receives improved boot hinge design, giving better access and hiding external hinges.
2000	Digital odometer replaces mechanical version. TVR announces Griffith production will cease following the completion of 100 SE (special edition) cars. Chassis now coated light grey, as per the newer 'T-Cars.'
2001	Chimaera 400 and 500 cease production.
2002	Final Griffith 500SE produced.
2003	Final Chimaera 450 produced.

(Courtesy K Bamber)

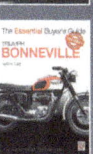

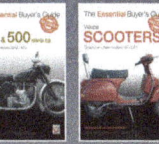

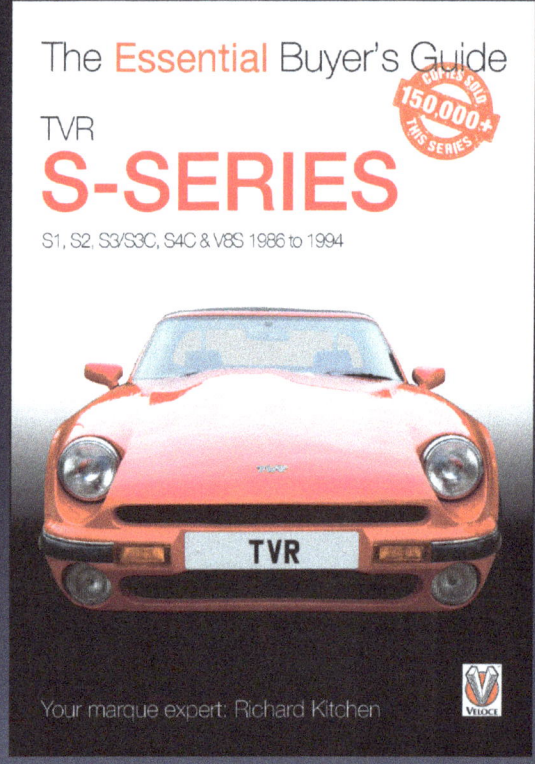

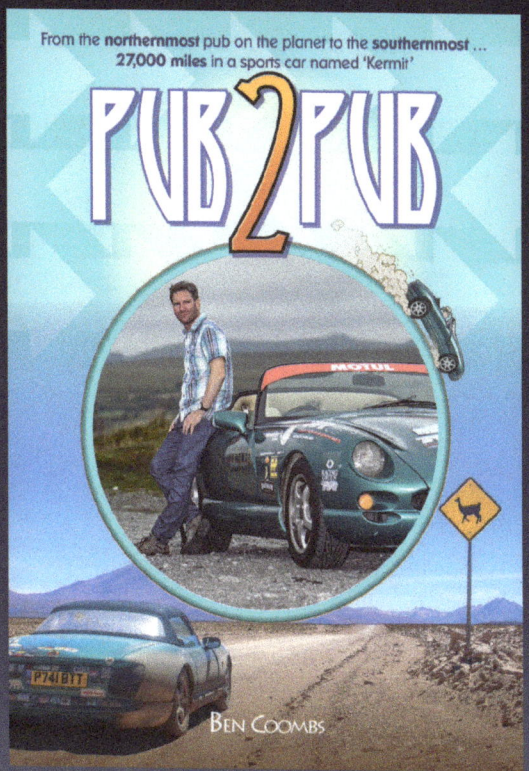

A gloriously British blend of elegance and eccentricity, *Pub2Pub* is the official account of the longest journey ever made by a British sports car – a 27,000 mile odyssey from the northernmost bar on the planet, to the southernmost, crossing countries, continents and cultures.

ISBN: 978-1-787113-60-2
Paperback • 21x14.8cm • 240 pages • 80 colour pictures

For more information and price details, visit our website at www.veloce.co.uk •
email: info@veloce.co.uk • Tel: +44(0)1305 260068

Index

Notes

Notes